Cambridge Elements ≡

Elements in Phonology
edited by
Robert Kennedy
University of California, Santa Barbara
Patrycja Strycharczuk
University of Manchester

QUANTITATIVE AND COMPUTATIONAL APPROACHES TO PHONOLOGY

Jane Chandlee
Haverford College

CAMBRIDGE
UNIVERSITY PRESS

Shaftesbury Road, Cambridge CB2 8EA, United Kingdom

One Liberty Plaza, 20th Floor, New York, NY 10006, USA

477 Williamstown Road, Port Melbourne, VIC 3207, Australia

314–321, 3rd Floor, Plot 3, Splendor Forum, Jasola District Centre,
New Delhi – 110025, India

103 Penang Road, #05–06/07, Visioncrest Commercial, Singapore 238467

Cambridge University Press is part of Cambridge University Press & Assessment,
a department of the University of Cambridge.

We share the University's mission to contribute to society through the pursuit of
education, learning and research at the highest international levels of excellence.

www.cambridge.org
Information on this title: www.cambridge.org/9781009539449

DOI: 10.1017/9781009420402

When citing this work, please include a reference to the DOI 10.1017/9781009420402

First published 2024

A catalogue record for this publication is available from the British Library.

ISBN 978-1-009-53944-9 Hardback
ISBN 978-1-009-42039-6 Paperback
ISSN 2633-9064 (online)
ISSN 2633-9056 (print)

Quantitative and Computational Approaches to Phonology

Elements in Phonology

DOI: 10.1017/9781009420402
First published online: November 2024

Jane Chandlee
Haverford College

Author for correspondence: Jane Chandlee, jchandlee@haverford.edu

Abstract: This Element surveys the various lines of work that have applied algorithmic, formal, mathematical, statistical, and/or probabilistic methods to the study of phonology and the computational problems it solves. Topics covered include: how quantitative and/or computational methods have been used in research on both rule- and constraint-based theories of grammar, including questions about how grammars are learned from data; how to best account for gradience as observed in acceptability judgments and the relative frequencies of different structures in the lexicon; what formal language theory, model theory, and information theory can and have contributed to the study of phonology; and what new directions in connectionist modeling are being explored. The overarching goal is to highlight how the work grounded in these various methods and theoretical orientations is distinct but also interconnected, and how central quantitative and computational approaches have become to the research in and teaching of phonology.

Keywords: computational, quantitative, phonology, learning, models

ISBNs: 9781009539449 (HB), 9781009420396 (PB), 9781009420402 (OC)
ISSNs: 2633-9064 (online), 2633-9056 (print)

Contents

1 Introduction

At first glance, combining the vast and diverse areas of quantitative *and* computational phonology in a single survey seems like a daunting task.[1] But even a little reflection reveals the necessity of this combination, as establishing an agreed-upon dividing line between these areas is neither possible nor particularly useful. For example, what makes an approach to phonology a "computational" one? Perhaps it means the use of software to implement and/or test a particular model, analysis, or learning algorithm. But this definition omits or at least misconstrues work grounded in a formal theory of the nature of computation that maintains a distinction between algorithm and code. Taking this idea even further, we might consider *all* work on phonology to be computational in nature, given that the phonology itself is a computational system that solves a variety of problems such as recognition (parsing an overt form), generation (mapping an underlying form to a surface form), and membership (assessing well-formedness). Furthermore, since a phonological grammar is the end target of acquisition, any work that theorizes or characterizes that grammar relates to some version of the phonological learning problem.

The term "quantitative" likewise invokes multiple associations, from the gradient nature of phonological patterns themselves, to the stochastic or nondeterministic algorithms used to model them, to the statistical methods that compare the resulting models to each other. In practice, research grounded in all of these ideas is of course aided by computational tools. The strategy behind this Element, then, is to instead embrace this entanglement and to celebrate the innovation and enthusiasm of scholars who have applied algorithmic, formal, mathematical, statistical, and/or probabilistic methods to the study of phonology and the computational problems it solves. This goal of course provides an enormous amount of ground to cover, and so an additional inclusion criterion is a shared assumption of an abstract phonological grammar in the generative tradition (broadly construed) that is distinct from – though not necessarily independent of – the phonetics. As a result, certain lines of work that are unequivocally computational and/or quantitative are regrettably being left out in the interest of space limitations and narrative cohesion. These include (among others) the learning of phonetic categories (e.g., Dillon et al. 2013; Thorburn et al. 2022; Matusevych et al. 2023), the modeling of lexical acquisition via phonetic variation (e.g., Elsner et al. 2012, 2013), and usage-based and exemplar models of phonology (e.g., Bybee 2001, 2007; Pierrehumbert 2001a, 2001b).

For the areas that will be covered, the objective is to be representative rather than exhaustive, in order to demonstrate the myriad ways that quantitative and

---

[1] And it was.

computational approaches have been applied to a variety of questions grounded in a variety of theoretical perspectives. To that end, the organizational structure is a combination of methods, theories, and problems of interest. Specifically, the outline of the Element is as follows. Section 2 discusses computational work on rule-based phonological grammars and how they are learned. Section 3 then reviews work on constraint-based phonology, with a focus on computational and probabilistic models for the learning of grammars and hidden structure.

Following these discussions of work grounded in phonological grammars of particular types, the next three sections show how these traditional core areas of research have been extended to address additional areas of interest through a variety of methods. Section 4 turns to a central area where quantitative methods have been employed: gradient acceptability and the contribution of lexical statistics to phonotactic generalizations. Section 5 briefly surveys the application of information theoretic methods to questions about phonological structure, and then Section 6 likewise briefly surveys the past, current, and potential future applications of connectionist models to the study of phonology. Stepping back, Section 7 discusses the contributions that formal language and model theoretic approaches to phonology can and have made to the study of phonological typology, learning, and representations. Rather than focusing on particular types of grammars, such work draws distinctions based on phonological patterns themselves, making its findings relevant to any theory of the phonological grammar and how it is learned. Finally, Section 8 concludes.

Importantly, these sectional groupings are not intended as a partition, as the boundary lines (both conceptual and methodological) are often blurry. The broader goal is instead to highlight how these categories complement each other and have great potential for further integration. These problems are hard. Studying them from as many angles as possible can only lead to greater collective progress on the many fascinating open questions about the phonological component of human languages.

2 Rule-Based Phonology

We begin with a discussion of formal approaches to *rule-based phonology*, a term most often defined in contrast to *constraint-based phonology*, which will be discussed in Section 3. The distinction between these categories is not absolute, as rule-based theories can and have made use of constraints (e.g., morpheme structure constraints, Halle 1959, Stanley 1967, or constraints that block or trigger a rule's application; see Reiss 2008 for examples and discussion). A set of rules can also function like constraints on input–output mappings, as in Koskenniemi's (1983) theory of two-level rules. Furthermore, the term *rule* is sometimes used to refer to a context-dependent pattern of alternation between segments. To "learn a phonological rule" can mean to learn the fact that, for example, {t, d} in American English are flapped between two vowels, or {p, t, k} are aspirated as simple onsets. The use of "rule" here is just a shorthand for a type of pattern and is not necessarily tied to any particular assumption about the form of the phonological grammar.

The scope of this section includes work that does make such an assumption, namely that the phonological grammar consists of a set of ordered context-sensitive rules. Two main threads of research will be discussed. The first is work on formalizing such grammars, including specifying the algorithm by which a rule applies to a string. The second is work on the learning of these grammars.

Arguably, the first theory that comes to mind in the context of rule-based phonology is the one proposed in Chomsky and Halle's (1968) *Sound Pattern of English* (hereafter SPE), in which phonological rules take the form in (1):

(1)　　　$A \rightarrow B / X \_ Y$

This rule asserts that A is rewritten as B when in the context X__Y (i.e., the string XAY is rewritten XBY). However, the extension of such a rule (i.e., the set of input–output string pairs it represents) is ambiguous without a specification for how the rule applies to a string. This ambiguity is most apparent with rules and strings that have the potential for multiple applications. Consider the rule in (2a) and the string in (2b); depending on *how* the rule applies, the output for this string could be [par], [pa], etcetera.

(2)　　　a. $[+\text{cons}] \rightarrow \emptyset / \_ \#$
　　　　　b. /park/

The rule application algorithm specified in SPE has become known as *simultaneous application* and is stated as follows: "To apply a rule, the entire string is first scanned for segments that satisfy the environmental constraints of the rule. After all such segments have been identified in the string, the changes required by the rule are applied simultaneously" (Chomsky and Halle 1968: 344). Assuming this algorithm, the rule in (2a) maps /park/ to [par], since in the underlying representation (UR) only /k/ satisfies the rule's structural description ([+cons]#).

Johnson (1972) provides a formal argument for why simultaneous rules are preferable to iterative ones, where an iterative rule is defined as one that applies repeatedly to a string as long as any targets remain. Specifically, he proves that iterative rules can simulate any arbitrary string rewriting system, while simultaneous ones are limited to the power of finite-state transducers (FSTs). He then goes on to develop a theory of linear rules, which – like iterative rules – can apply multiple times to a string, but – like simultaneous rules – are limited to the expressivity of finite-state. Their restrictiveness comes from a requirement that each successive application moves further into the string, in contrast to iterative rules for which there is no imposed order on the different applications. In other words, linear rules are *directional* and are specified to apply either left to right or right to left.

Despite their formal equivalence, linear rules are argued to be preferable to simultaneous ones on account of the greater simplicity with which they can capture multiple applications. Simultaneous rules do allow for multiple applications through the mechanism of parenthesis-star, by which a rule becomes an abbreviation for an infinite set of rules that contain zero or more tokens of the expression in parentheses. Consider the example ATR harmony rule in (3a). Simultaneous application will only identify the first /ʊ/ as a target in (3b), with the resulting output [putukʊ].

(3)   a. $V \rightarrow [+ATR]/[+ATR]\,C_0$—
        b. /putʊkʊ/ → [putukʊ]

If the actual surface form reflects an additional application (i.e., [putuku]), the rule can be instead formulated as in (4a). This version represents an infinite set of rules, including (3a) as well as (4b) and (4c), that allows for zero or more [−ATR] vowels to intervene between the trigger and target. As long as a vowel satisfies one of the rules in this infinite expansion in the UR, it will harmonize to [+ATR] under simultaneous application (i.e., the second /ʊ/ in (3b) satisfies rule (4b)).

(4)   a. $V \rightarrow [+ATR]/[+ATR]\,C_0([-ATR]\,C_0)^*$—
        b. $V \rightarrow [+ATR]/[+ATR]\,C_0[-ATR]\,C_0$—
        c. $V \rightarrow [+ATR]/[+ATR]\,C_0[-ATR]\,C_0[-ATR]\,C_0$—

As a linear rule that applies left to right, however, (3a) can achieve the same effect without the added notation of parenthesis-star. After the first application generates [putukʊ], the newly created [u] can serve as the trigger for the final vowel. Johnson's work thus provided a formal grounding from which to compare theories of rules and rule application in terms of both descriptive adequacy and elegance.[2]

We turn now to the question of learning rules and rule-based grammars. From the perspective of formal learnability, such grammars do not have many inherent advantages. Context-sensitive grammars like SPE are not learnable from positive data; indeed (as will be discussed further in Section 7), not even regular

---

[2] For more discussion and comparison of rule-application algorithms, see Howard (1972), Anderson (1974), and Kenstowicz and Kisseberth (1977, 1979). See also Bale and Reiss's (2018) textbook, which introduces phonology through the formal syntax and semantics of SPE-style grammars.

grammars are, despite being situated well below context-sensitive on the Chomsky–Schützenberger hierarchy (Chomsky 1959; Chomsky and Schützenberger 1959):

(5)   Finite ⊂ Regular ⊂ Context-free ⊂ Context-sensitive ⊂ Recursively enumerable

Early work on rule learning then focused on the question of how a learner can identify the correct rule or grammar when more than one are descriptively adequate. Johnson (1984) demonstrates a deductive approach to learning a limited set of phonological rules of the form in (6), where "a" and "b" are segments and "C" is a feature matrix of unspecified length that is a subset of the segments surrounding "a."

(6) $a \rightarrow b/C$

The input data is a set of paradigms with stems inflected with various affixes. Through inspection of this data, the learner identifies the contexts in which "a" alternates with "b" without including those tokens of "a" that do not alternate. In the case of multiple ordered rules, it entertains all possible hypotheses for which alternation took place last, undoes that discovered rule, and then repeats this procedure until all alternations have been accounted for. The procedure is error driven in the sense that it rejects a hypothesis when it arrives at a point where the rule discovery procedure fails. This working-backward technique means the learner will also propose URs for the stems and affixes present in the data.

Johnson's approach demonstrates that the presence of non-surface-true patterns resulting from rule ordering is not inherently a barrier to learning, but additional selection criteria are needed for such a learner to converge on a single grammar. In a case in which the rules are not strictly ordered (i.e., multiple orderings will correctly generate the data), the learner will identify multiple grammars with no way of deciding among them. Similarly, given that the context of a single rule will not always be strongly data determined, the learner will need to appeal to some type of evaluation metric or guiding principle to select among a set of adequate contexts.

Other work that addresses the learnability of rules has been couched in a *substance-free* theory that emphasizes the formal nature of phonology as a computational system that operates over symbolic representations. Reiss (2008: 258–9) – summarizing views presented in earlier work including Hale and Reiss (2000a, 2000b) – articulates the substance-free view of the phonological system as follows:

> The computational system treats features as arbitrary symbols. What this means is that many of the so-called phonological universals (often discussed under the rubric of markedness) are in fact epiphenomena deriving from the interaction of extragrammatical factors like acoustic salience and the nature

of language change. Phonology is not and should not be grounded in phonetics since the facts which phonetic grounding is meant to explain can be derived without reference to phonology.[3]

This focus on phonological computation enables a streamlined conception of universal grammar (UG) that facilitates formal discussions and treatments of learning problems. For example, Dell (1981) discusses the subset problem inherent to the learning of optional rules. As an example, French optionally deletes an /l/ that follows an obstruent and precedes a consonant or pause:

(7)   a. /kɛltabl/ → [kɛltabl] ~ [kɛltab], *quelle table?*, "which table?"
       b. /parl/ → [parl](*[par]), *parle*, "speak"

Consider two versions of this deletion rule: Deletion A targets coda /l/'s following obstruents, and Deletion B targets coda /l/'s following any consonant. The evidence that distinguishes these two rules is negative evidence, such as the ungrammaticality of *[par] in (7b). But given that such evidence is unavailable to the French-learning child, how do they come to select Deletion A instead of Deletion B? This is the subset problem. The grammar that includes the less restrictive Deletion B will correctly generate all of the observed data. Without negative evidence, the learner will never have reason to consider a more restrictive grammar (i.e., one that generates a proper subset of the forms generated by its current grammar). Dell then proposes that the language acquisition device (LAD) must include the strategy of always selecting the more restrictive grammar when faced with this choice.

Notably, this scenario is only relevant to the case of optional rules. As an optional rule, Deletion A generates the language including [tabl], [tab], and [parl], while the less restrictive Deletion B generates [tabl], [tab], [parl], and *[par]. But if the rules are obligatory, the subset–superset relationship no longer holds: Deletion A generates [tab] and [parl] while Deletion B generates [tab] and *[par]. In this case, positive data – specifically, encountering [parl] – will be sufficient to correct an earlier hypothesis of Deletion B. In this way, obligatory rules serve to provide indirect negative evidence (i.e., if [parl] is grammatical, then *[par] must not be). The challenge, of course, is how the learner can know whether the rule they are learning is optional or obligatory. To address this issue, Dell further proposes that the learner assumes the rule is obligatory until they encounter evidence of optionality.

Hale and Reiss (2008) recast the subset principle as a description of the learner's initial state, rather than a guiding principle for selecting among

---

[3] See a recent special issue of the *Canadian Journal of Linguistics/Revue canadienne de linguistique* (Volume 67 Number 4) for a collection of papers situated in this approach.

competing grammars. In particular, they argue that UG must provide the complete set of primitives (i.e., features) so that the learner can posit the most specified rule possible (contra typically assumed pressures of economy in rule formulations) that accounts for all and only the forms to which it applies. Generalizing over observed instances of the rule is achieved via set intersection over the fully specified feature bundles. Maximally specifying while still generalizing is necessary for the reasons stated earlier in this Element: an overly general rule will never be contradicted by positive evidence alone.

This principle of generalizing over more specified instances was employed in the minimal generalization learner of Albright and Hayes (2002, 2003), who investigate rule learning in the context of the rules-versus-analogy debate of inflectional morphology (e.g., Pinker and Prince 1994; Bybee 2001).[4] The learner compares pairs of (present, past) forms to identify the change that derives the past from the present. For example, the comparison of *shine* and *shined* reveals the rule in (8):

(8)   Ø → d / ʃaɪn__

This rule is, of course, overly specific, but additional comparisons reveal more rules that share its structural change (e.g., *grab-grabbed, hug-hugged, fill-filled*, etc.). The specifications of these rules can be combined into the more general rule in (9a), or using features, (9b).

(9)   a. Ø → d / {n, b, g, l}__
           b. Ø → d / [+cons, +voice]__

This procedure will generate a set of rules that differ in their generality, such that a given input may be subject to more than one rule. To address this ambiguity, all rules are also given a confidence score, which is the number of forms in the training data that the rule *correctly* applies to (i.e., its number of hits) divided by the number of forms it *can* apply to (i.e., the rule's scope). The set of rules along with their confidence scores can account for gradience (see Section 4) if an output's well-formedness is taken as the score of the "best" rule that generates it.

Getting back to the question of the learner's initial state, Hale and Reiss's (2008) argument is that because the distinctions needed to work out the phonological system can only be detected to the extent that parsing encodes forms differently, the maximally specified initial representation needed to avoid the subset problem is only possible if UG provides all features. But Odden (2022) rejects this assumption in favor of *radical* substance-free phonology, in which

---

[4] Minimal generalization as a learning strategy is not dependent on the rule formalism. It is also used to inform the learning of phonotactic constraints in Albright (2009), which will be discussed in Section 4.

only the abstract concept of a feature is provided by UG rather than an actual feature set. The learning of both the feature set and the rules of the grammar is guided by the evidence of how and which sounds pattern together (see also Mielke 2008).[5] Even though the phonological system is responsible for parsing those sounds that are recognized as linguistic objects, the auditory system deals with acoustic representations of all sounds. If the current hypothesis for the phonological grammar has discarded important information about, for example, which sounds contrast, that information is still available through the auditory system and so a correction can be made. Given that, the learner's objective can be characterized by something other than avoiding the subset problem. Odden's (2022: 526) proposal instead emphasizes simplicity: "The task of feature acquisition is finding the simplest system of properties that accounts for those cases of grammatical functioning-together that can be observed in the primary linguistic data."

The significance of both restrictiveness *and* simplicity is recognized by Rasin et al. (2020, 2021), who argue that the learner's task is actually to find the optimal balance between these potentially conflicting demands. Specifically, they propose the use of minimum description length (MDL) for learning not just a grammar of ordered rewrite rules but also the lexicon of URs.[6] Length in this case is the combined total (in bits) of the grammar itself as well as the encoding of the data given that grammar. Consider again the example of optional /l/ deletion in French. The context-free version of this rule in (10a) is shorter than the target version in (10b), and so would be favored by simplicity.

(10)   a. $l \rightarrow \emptyset$
         b. $l \rightarrow \emptyset / [-son]\_\#$

Of course (10a) will over-generate, but as discussed earlier in this section, the learner cannot recover from that error without negative evidence. Employing something like the subset principle is necessary to select the correct rule.

However, Rasin et al. argue that the optionality of the rule creates a further problem. If the learner has only encountered one of the possible rule outputs – say either [tab] or [tabl] for "table" – then a grammar that does *not* generalize to predict the other form will be more restrictive than the one that includes (10b). One such grammar would be the one that does not propose a rule at all, but instead just lists in the lexicon all of the forms observed so far. In this way, the subset principle's insistence on restrictiveness can have the effect of preventing generalization.

---

[5] A substance-free approach is also compatible with non-rule-based formalisms; see Blaho (2008) for an approach to learning optimality theory constraints in this framework.
[6] See Goldsmith (2001, 2006) for earlier work using MDL to learn morphology.

Minimum description length balances these competing demands by computing not just the size of the grammar, but the "cost" of describing the data with that grammar. In particular, the cost of choosing a UR from the lexicon increases with the size of the lexicon (2 choices = 1 bit, 4 choices = 2 bits, etc.), and so generalizing with a rule is cheaper. In addition, whether or not an optional rule has applied to a UR that it can apply to is specified with an additional bit. (This added bit is not needed for obligatory rules, because whether or not they apply is determined by the choice of UR itself.) As an optional rule, then, (10b) is actually cheaper than (10a) because it can apply to fewer URs.

As the recency of Rasin et al.'s (2020, 2021) work shows, the question of how to learn rule-based grammars has not been abandoned, but it is undeniable that the progress in phonological learning research was greatly accelerated following the shift to constraint-based grammars like optimality theory (OT) (Prince and Smolensky 1993, 2004). The next section turns to the research on these grammar types, the comparisons among them, and how to learn them.

3 Constraint-Based Phonology

Constraint-based phonology has become an umbrella term for a collection of phonological theories that centralize constraints on representations instead of the procedures by which those representations are changed.[7] Given how readily these theories lend themselves to computational learning models and statistical methods for working with quantitative data and patterns, it is not surprising that the shift in the field from rule- to constraint-based phonology corresponded to a surge in research on these areas that continues today. This section will begin with an overview of different types of constraint-based grammars (Section 3.1), followed by a survey of the work addressing a variety of phonological learning problems (Section 3.2). Lastly, Section 3.3 will highlight some of the arguments used to compare these theories to each other, including their ability to address questions of theoretical interest as well as what is known about their respective complexity and learnability.

3.1 Constraint-Based Theories of Phonology

The theory of declarative phonology (Bird et al. 1992; Bird 1995) forgoes derivation in favor of inviolable (i.e., "hard") constraints whose interaction is compositional: all constraints must be satisfied simultaneously for a phonological object to be licit. The term *declarative* invokes the distinction between

---

[7] This centralization of constraints does not preclude the use of derivation, as exemplified by theories like stratal OT (Bermúdez-Otero 1999) and harmonic serialism (McCarthy 2000), but those theories maintain the emphasis on constraints over processes.

declarative and imperative programming languages, the former emphasizing the logic of the computation over the step-by-step procedure that performs it. Logic also provides a formal description language for the constraints themselves, which can be stated using predicates and logical connectives. For example, the constraint in (11) asserts that every onset is dominated by (∂) a syllable (example from Scobbie et al. 1996):

(11) $\forall x [onset(x) \rightarrow \exists y [syllable(y) \wedge \partial(y,x)]]$

What we might call a rule can also be represented with a constraint in the same description language – for example, (12), which says a high back vowel is specified as [+round]. Further conditions can be added to the antecedent to constrain this specification to certain contexts.

(12) $\forall x [[high(x) \wedge back(x)] \rightarrow round(x)]$

Lastly, morphemes or lexical entries are also stated as constraints (or partial descriptions), in contrast to more typical generative assumptions that differentiate the lexicon from the grammar that operates on it. For example, (13) gives a partial description of a vowel:

(13) $\exists x [high(x) \wedge back(x)]$

Declarative phonology has been applied to the study of many types of phonological structure; for examples see Broe (1993), Bird and Ellison (1994), and Scobbie et al. (1996), and references therein.

Inviolable constraints are language-particular and at times need to be quite specific in order to capture the context-dependent nature of phonological alternations and feature licensing. In contrast, *violable* constraints can be more general and amenable to arguments of a universal constraint set. However, the potential for violation necessitates a different mechanism than full satisfaction to determine well-formedness. One such mechanism is to rank the constraints in order of importance (or severity of violation), which is the foundation of OT.

As a basic example, the grammar in Table 1 shows how a word-final devoicing pattern can be represented in OT. Columns after the first one are labeled with members of the universal constraint set CON, and rows after the first one are labeled with one of the infinite set of candidate surface forms provided by GEN. Cells are filled in by EVAL, which assesses whether and to what extent each candidate violates each constraint.

The UR /bad/ violates the *markedness* constraint *D#, which says words cannot end in voiced obstruents. The winning candidate (marked with ☞), also violates a constraint, the *faithfulness* constraint Ident(voice), which says that

Table 1 Optimality theory grammar for final devoicing

UR: /bad/	DEP	MAX	*D#	Ident(voice)
[bad]			*!	
☞[bat]				*
[ba]		*!		
[bada]	*!			

surface specifications of the feature voice should match their underlying values. But because the constraints are ranked in order of importance (with left-to-right corresponding to more-to-less important), the violation of Ident(voice) is less serious than the violation of *D#, and so [bat] is the optimal form among those evaluated. Additional faithfulness constraints that are violated by other means of avoiding the violation of *D# – including deleting the obstruent (MAX = don't delete) or adding a word-final vowel (DEP = don't add) – must also be ranked above Ident(voice) so as to ensure the candidate that violates it is in fact the winner.

"Classic" OT grammars are categorical, mapping an input to its single, optimal output. But there is great interest in models of grammar that allow for multiple outputs due to variation, as well as account for the observed gradience in acceptability judgments and/or lexical statistics (as will be discussed at length in the next section). Proposals for modeling gradience with a grammar of ranked constraints have included (1) stochastic OT, (2) partially ordered constraints, and (3) the rank-ordered model of EVAL. These will now be discussed in turn.[8]

In stochastic OT (Boersma 1997; Boersma and Hayes 2001), constraints are associated with a range of values rather than a fixed position. During evaluation, a random variable introduces noise that establishes each constraint's position in its respective range, and then all constraints are ranked according to these selected positions. If two constraints have nonoverlapping ranges, it amounts to a fixed ranking between them. With overlapping ranges, the respective ranking of two constraints will vary in a way that reflects how often different candidates surface as the winner for a given UR. For instance, if in the provided example final devoicing is optional, the two candidates [bad] and [bat] could surface in proportion to how often the positions of *D# and Ident(voice) are reversed in the ranking order. While the grammar is still categorical, gradient

---

[8] These solutions still have to address the all-or-nothing problem that arises when a given form has multiple potential application sites for an optional process (see Riggle and Wilson 2006 and Vaux 2008). Thanks to a reviewer for pointing this out.

well-formedness can be captured in terms of the percentage of some number of trials in which a particular form wins.[9]

Another approach to handling optionality in OT is the use of partial orders of constraints. In the example grammar in Table 1, the constraints are actually in a partial, not strict, order because the relative ranking of DEP, MAX, and *D# is irrelevant to selecting the winner. This partial order, shown in (14), can be cashed out into multiple strict orders, some of which are listed in (15).

(14)   {DEP, MAX, *D#} ≫ Ident(voice)

(15)   a. DEP ≫ MAX ≫ *D# ≫ Ident(voice)
         b. DEP ≫ *D# ≫ MAX ≫ Ident(voice)
         c. MAX ≫ DEP ≫ *D# ≫ Ident(voice)

In the case of optionality, multiple output forms are possible as long as they win under at least one of the strict orders allowed by the grammar's partial order. Anttila (1997a, 1997b) demonstrates this potential with the complex patterns of Finnish noun inflections. For example, the genitive form of /maailma/, "world" varies between the "strong" and "weak" forms in (16a) and (16b) (acute and grave accents indicate primary and secondary stress, respectively).

(16)   /maailma/, "world"
         a. [máa.il.mòi.den]
         b. [máa.il.mo.jen]

In Anttila's analysis, NoClash allows for alternating syllables to be stressed, but secondary stress is optional. The two outputs in (16) tie on the weight-to-stress constraints *Ĺ and *H (i.e., neither violates the former and both violate the latter once). This indeterminacy of the grammar explains why both forms are permitted, as well as their observed frequency of occurrence (~50/50). Optionality is also predicted when two candidates do not tie but disagree on constraints that are not strictly ordered. This is the case for the stem /naapuri/, "neighbor," which has the possible output forms shown in (17a) and (17b).

(17)   /naapuri/, "neighbor"
         a. [náa.pu.rèi.den]
         b. [náa.pu.ri.en]

Candidate (17a) violates *H/I (weight–sonority harmony) and *Í (stress–sonority harmony), while candidate (17b) violates *L.L (no lapse). But both are able to surface because this set of constraints {*H/I, *Í, *L.L} is not in a strict order.

---

[9] See also Hammond (2003, 2004) for probabilistic OT, in which the probabilistic ranking of each markedness constraint with regard to faithfulness is assumed to be independent, and gradient acceptability reflects the joint probabilities of the rankings of the relevant markedness constraints.

Which one actually surfaces is determined by random selection of one of the possible strict orders of these three constraints. Furthermore, the probability of each form can be determined as the proportion of possible orders it wins under. In this example, (17a) wins whenever the two constraints it violates are ranked below the one constraint violated by (17b). The ratio of four orders under which (17b) wins to two orders under which (17a) wins corresponds closely to their observed frequencies in a corpus analysis.

Lastly, Coetzee's (2006) proposal attributes variation to the way constraints are evaluated instead of the way they are ranked. In this rank-ordering model of EVAL, relative grammaticality can be assessed even among the nonoptimal candidates that do not win. Consider again Table 1, and assume (for the sake of demonstration) that MAX, DEP, and *D# are strictly ordered as shown. Putting aside the winning candidate [bat], the remaining candidates can be ordered according to the ranking of the constraint they fatally violate: [bad] is more well-formed than [ba], which is in turn more well formed than [bada]. The consequent prediction is that the higher a candidate appears in this order, the more frequent it will be. Limits on variation are imposed with a "cutoff" point in the constraint ranking, such that variation is only possible among candidates whose well-formedness is determined by constraints below the cutoff.

Another prominent approach to variation is the use of a constraint set that is *weighted* instead of ranked, as in OT's predecessor harmonic grammar (HG) (Legendre et al. 1990; Smolensky and Legendre 2006). With weighted constraints, candidates are assessed using the weighted sum of constraint violations, called the *harmony score*:

(18) $$H = \sum_{k=1}^{K} w_k \cdot s_k$$

In (18), w_k is the weight of constraint k, and s_k is the number of violations (typically represented with negative numbers). The optimal candidate is the one with greatest harmony, or the score closest to zero. Table 2 presents an HG version of the grammar from Table 1 with MAX and DEP omitted for simplicity. The constraint weights are listed at the top of each column and the candidates' harmony scores are listed at the end of each row.

Table 2 Harmonic grammar for final devoicing

weights:	2	1	
UR: /bad/	***D#**	**Ident(voice)**	**Harmony:**
[bad]	−1		−2
☞[bat]		−1	−1

One advantage of HG is its ability to model the cumulative effects of violating multiple constraints, in contrast to OT in which only violations of the highest-ranked decisive constraint matter. (More will be said about cumulativity in Section 3.3.) But the grammar is still categorical and outputs a single optimal form. To address variation, Noisy HG (Boersma and Pater 2016) adds random noise to the constraint weights during evaluation:

(19) $\qquad H = \sum_{k=1}^{K} (w_k + N_k) \cdot s_k$

In (19), N is a random variable sampled from a Gaussian distribution. The use of noise to adjust constraint weights allows for potentially different outputs to emerge as optimal, but each time the grammar is used there is still only one output. In contrast, a maximum entropy (MaxEnt) HG grammar produces multiple outputs in the form of a probability distribution over the candidate set. The conditional probability of each candidate y given a UR x is calculated by raising the base of the natural logarithm to the candidate's harmony score ($H(y)$) and normalizing over all candidates under consideration, Y (Goldwater and Johnson 2003).

(20) $\qquad P(x) = \dfrac{1}{Z(x)} \, exp \, H(y)$

(21) $\qquad Z(x) = \sum_{y \in Y(x)} exp \, H(y)$

The constraint weights are identified with maximum likelihood estimation: the goal is to find the weights that maximize the product of the conditional probabilities of all input–output pairs in the training corpus. This learning objective is a particular conception of the phonological learning problem, one that is tied to the initial assumption about what form the phonological grammar takes. The next section will explore this connection between grammar and learning problems further by discussing the phonological learning literature grounded in the previously described constraint-based theories.

3.2 Learning with Constraint-Based Grammars

As with rule-based grammars, a central question for constraint-based grammars is how they are learned from positive data. This section will survey the various ways this question has been addressed, which include different formulations of the learning problem itself. Section 3.2.1 starts with work that assumes the constraint set is known in advance – either as a simplifying assumption or because it is provided by UG – and therefore the learning problem is a matter of identifying the correct ranking of these provided constraints. Section 3.2.2 addresses the problems inherent to learning from surface forms alone, which include the learning of hidden structure and underlying forms. Lastly, Section 3.2.3 turns to the problem of learning the constraints themselves.

3.2.1 Learning Constraint Rankings

Under the assumption that the phonological grammar is a set of ranked constraints and the constraints themselves are provided by UG, the learning problem is to identify the correct ranking of those constraints for the target language. One advantage of defining the learning problem in this way is that the logic of optimization provides implicit negative evidence in the form of the candidates that do not win. Influential work by Tesar (1995) and Tesar and Smolensky (1993, 1996, 1998, 2000) demonstrated how this evidence can be used with an algorithm called recursive constraint demotion (RCD).

Recursive constraint demotion makes use of winner–loser pairs of candidates to produce a stratified hierarchy of groups of constraints, in which constraints in the same group do not conflict with one another.[10] Returning to the final devoicing example, Table 3 is a comparative tableau (Prince 2000) for pairs of candidates (the first being the desired winner) with indicators of which constraints prefer the winning candidate (W) or the losing candidate (L). Constraint preference here refers to which candidate violates the constraint to a lesser degree; blank cells indicate that the candidates tie on that constraint.

The basic logic of optimization is that the constraints that favor losing candidates must be outranked by at least one constraint that favors the winner. To achieve this, RCD first identifies those constraints that prefer only winners and situates them in the top stratum of the hierarchy. In this example, those constraints are *D#, MAX, and DEP. Winner–loser pairs that are accounted for with this ranking can then be removed, and the process repeats with the remaining pairs and constraints. With this simple example, all winner–loser pairs are accounted for after the first pass, leaving the ranking of {*D#, MAX, DEP} ≫ Ident(voice) as desired.

With respect to the subset problem discussed in Section 2, identifying the subset relations among grammars of ranked constraints becomes increasingly

Table 3 Comparative tableau based on the example grammar
in Table 1

UR: /bad/	Ident(voice)	*D#	MAX	DEP
bat ~ bad	L	W		
bat ~ ba			W	
bat ~ bada				W

---

[10] See Tesar and Smolensky (1998, 2000) for an error-driven approach to identifying informative winner–loser pairs, and Tesar (1998) for an online version of RCD (multi-RCD) that shows how learning can proceed over time.

infeasible as the size of the assumed constraint set grows (i.e., there are $k!$ possible grammars for a set of k constraints). Instead, the search for the most restrictive grammar consistent with the observed data has been addressed through the relative ranking of markedness constraints with respect to faithfulness constraints. Consider the (simplified) example of learning stress patterns as in the PAKA system defined by Tesar et al. (2003). Following richness of the base (Prince and Smolensky 1993), underlying forms can be either stressed or unstressed, and the constraints in question include the markedness constraint StressLeftmost (first syllable is stressed) and the faithfulness constraint Ident (stress) (preserve underlying values for stress). The ranking of markedness over faithfulness (StressLeftmost ≫ Ident(stress)) is the most restrictive: all underlying contrasts for the feature stress collapse to the predictable pattern of first syllable stress. The ranking of faithfulness over markedness (Ident(stress) ≫ StressLeftmost) is the least restrictive in that all underlying contrasts are preserved.

More generally, a grammar's degree of restrictiveness can be assessed in terms of how many markedness constraints dominate faithfulness constraints. Prince and Tesar (2004) call this the *r-measure*, with a larger r-measure corresponding to a more restrictive grammar. But now consider that in the case of phonotactic learning – in which the UR is assumed to be identical to the surface representation, or SR (more on this in the next section) – faithfulness constraints are effectively inviolable. Since RCD ranks constraints as high as possible, faithfulness constraints will end up at the top of the hierarchy at great cost to the r-measure. Prince and Tesar's (2004) proposed solution is *biased constraint demotion* (BCD), in which faithfulness constraints are only situated into the hierarchy when no markedness constraints are available.[11] The consequence is a delay in ranking faithfulness constraints that maximizes the resulting grammar's r-measure, as desired.

In the case of stochastic OT, the learning problem is not to learn a fixed ranking, but the range of values associated with each constraint. The gradual learning algorithm (GLA) proposed by Boersma (1997) and Boersma and Hayes (2001) assumes these ranges are Gaussian distributions (with a fixed standard deviation) that are centered on a constraint-specific *ranking value*, in which case the target of learning is to identify these ranking values. The learner is error-driven and makes use of (UR, SR) pairs for which the current hypothesis of the grammar selects an incorrect winner as the SR. A constraint that is violated by the actual SR but not the incorrect winner is moved down the

---

[11] See also Hayes (2004) for an independent proposal of a similar algorithm and Tessier (2007, 2009) for a use of BCD in a gradual, *error-selective* learner that can model the stages of phonological acquisition.

scale, while a constraint violated by the incorrect winner but not the actual SR is moved up the scale. These movements are by a fixed amount, called the plasticity.

Stochastic OT's ability to handle variation means it can learn from noisy data that not only reflects optionality but also includes speech errors. When the same UR appears with multiple SRs in the training data, each token will have an effect on the ranking values of the relevant constraints. The resulting grammar will then generate those forms in proportion with their frequency of occurrence in the data. In addition, as demonstrated by Zuraw (2000), stochastic ranking can account for lexical regularities that do not drive alternations and often have exceptions. With the GLA's method of adjusting ranking values, the more words that violate a constraint, the lower ranked it will be (and vice versa). The likelihood of a word being an exception is then captured by the degree of overlap among the relevant constraints.

To close this section, we will briefly discuss learning rankings in harmonic serialism (HS) (McCarthy 2000), a constraint-based framework that reintroduces the concept of derivation. In HS, the UR–SR mapping occurs in steps, with each step consisting of an OT-style selection of the optimal candidate according to a fixed ranking of constraints. The winning candidate becomes the input to the subsequent step, and GEN is restricted such that each candidate can differ from the input by only a single violation of a faithfulness constraint. The derivation concludes when the fully faithful candidate is selected as the winner.

As discussed by Tessier and Jesney (2014), HS's use of derivation introduces a challenge for error-driven learning in that the informative error may be hidden in one of the intermediate steps. To address this challenge, Tessier (2012) proposes a multistage learning process in which the ranking information that can be gleaned from the SR is later refined using the candidate set generated for observed forms, first to construct winner–loser pairs and then as hypothetical inputs to the grammar. Jarosz (2016) also addresses the problems inherent to learning derivations in the context of serial markedness reduction (SMR) (Jarosz 2014), a variant of HS proposed to handle opaque process interactions.

In SMR, candidates are annotated with which markedness constraints they satisfy, and additional serial markedness constraints are used to favor candidates that satisfy constraints in a particular order. To learn such grammars, Jarosz (2016) proposes expectation driven learning (EDL), a probabilistic learning approach that in this case assumes a stochastic version of Anttila's (1997a, 1997b) partial order grammars discussed previously in Section 3.1. The learner identifies the pairwise ranking probabilities of the constraints based on how often each ranking successfully generates the observed data. Because the learner considers each possible (pairwise, not total) ranking in turn, it does not need information about the intermediate steps of the derivation and uses only examples of the composite UR–SR mapping.

The intermediate steps of an HS derivation are one example of the *hidden structure* problem that has drawn a lot of attention in the phonological learning literature. Expectation driven learning and other probabilistic learning methods for constraint-based grammars have played a large role in this line of work, which will be explored further in the next section.

3.2.2 Learning Hidden Structure

The term *hidden structure* refers to information not available in the observable data that is nonetheless important for identifying the grammar that generated those forms. While providing a learner with full structural descriptions and/or (UR, SR) pairs can be a valuable simplifying assumption for making initial progress on phonological learning problems, the more realistic setup of learning from overt forms is the ultimate goal. This section will review some of the work that has drawn on constraint-based frameworks to take on that challenge.

One type of hidden structure is the ambiguity of syllable boundaries and metrical structure. Consider an overt form [apa], which could be syllabified in various ways, including [a.pa] and [ap.a]. Similarly, stress placement on the first vowel could result from a trochaic foot (ápa), or a degenerate foot followed by an extrametrical final syllable (á)<pa>. The correct parse depends on the grammar, but to learn that grammar the learner needs to know what the correct parse is. To address this circularity, Tesar and Smolensky (2000) incorporate robust interpretative parsing (RIP) into an iterative version of RCD. Starting from an assumed initial constraint hierarchy, RIP maps an overt form to its full structural description according to this grammar. The UR for that structural description is then mapped to its optimal SR, again according to the current grammar. If these two structural descriptions do not match, they are used as a winner–loser pair by RCD to revise the grammar. This parsing/production feedback loop iterates until there are no more mismatches.[12]

As a simple example, consider a target grammar that assigns penultimate stress by way of a right-aligned trochee. Now assume some (incorrect) constraint hierarchy that parses the overt form [σσσσσ] as [σσ(σσ́)σ]. That same grammar then parses the UR for this form, /σσσσσ/, as [(σσ́)σσσ]. Since these parses do not match – and further, the grammar's placement of stress contradicts what is actually observed – the learner knows that the hypothesized constraint hierarchy is wrong and needs to be adjusted. As with RCD more generally, the

---

[12] See Dresher and Kaye (1990) and Dresher (1999) for a comparison between RIP/CD and a cue-based learning approach for setting metrical parameters.

RIP/CD algorithm capitalizes on the implicit negative evidence of spurious winning forms, generating its own informative errors by using the same grammar for production and parsing.

Another source of the hidden structure problem is the lexicon of URs. The ranking of constraints that generates a UR–SR mapping depends on what the UR is, but the learner again only has access to overt forms. This interdependence of the grammar and the lexicon has been addressed in various ways. In the surgery learning algorithm (Tesar et al. 2003), when BCD runs into inconsistency in the set of winner–loser pairs – for example, if two constraints are left that have opposite winner–loser preferences – the learner uses that dead end as a cue that the lexicon must be modified. Lexicon updates target each (alternating) morpheme in turn until the inconsistency is resolved, after which the winner–loser pairs containing that morpheme are adjusted to reflect the change.

The interdependence problem has also been addressed by drawing on the learner's prior knowledge of phonotactics. Tesar and Prince (2007) explore this idea with an algorithm that first establishes a preliminary constraint ranking in a stage of phonotactic learning in which all URs are assumed to be identical to the SRs. Because we know the grammar accepts the SR, then *if* that SR were a UR we can assume the grammar would map it faithfully (since unfaithful mappings only occur when underlying structures cannot surface).

As an example, consider a target language in which codas are devoiced. A dataset of SRs for this language is given in (22). At this stage, the learner has no knowledge of morphological structure (i.e., all SRs are taken to be distinct and monomorphemic).

(22)   {tate, date, tade, dade, tat, dat}

Starting with the hierarchy in (23) in which all markedness outranks faithfulness, the learner uses BCD to find the most restrictive ranking that maps all SRs to themselves.[13] The form [dat], for example, presents a problem because its violation of *Voice makes it less harmonic than [tat] according to the initial ranking. Yet both are grammatical. Demoting *Voice below Ident(voice) solves this problem.

(23)   {*Voice, *SyllableFinalVoice, *IntervocalicVoiceless} ≫ Ident(voice)

And so on, until the learner arrives at the ranking in (24).

(24)   *SyllableFinalVoice ≫ Ident(voice) ≫ {*Voice, *IntervocalicVoiceless}

---

[13] This is a commonly held assumption about the initial state of the learner. See Smolensky (1996) for motivations and Hale and Reiss (1998) for counterarguments.

This preliminary ranking is then refined by bringing in knowledge of the morphological structure of the SRs and therefore witnessing alternations. The data at this point incorporates information about morpheme boundaries and identity:

(25) $\{tad_1\text{-}e_5, tat_2\text{-}e_5, dad_3\text{-}e_5, dat_4\text{-}e_5, tat_1, tat_2, dat_3, dat_4\}$

When a feature is observed to alternate, the learner considers all possible candidates for the UR. For example, the UR of morpheme 1 is either /tad/ or /tat/. With these hypotheses, the learner can test its current grammar (24) with the possible mappings in (26).

(26)   a. Hypothesis A : /tad/ → [tat] and /tade/ → [tade]
        b. Hypothesis B : /tat/ → [tat] and /tate/ → [tade]

As shown in Tables 4 and 5, Hypothesis A succeeds under the current constraint ranking, but Hypothesis B fails. The learner can thus conclude that Hypothesis A is correct and the UR is /tad/.

Stepping back, the broader intuition here is that the hypothesis that /tat/ is the UR can only succeed if this language has intervocalic voicing, a possibility ruled out by the phonotactics (i.e., the existence of [tate]). But the devoicing required by the UR /tad/ *is* consistent, since no SRs end in voiced obstruents.

Table 4 Testing Hypothesis A with grammar (24)

UR: /tad/	*SyllableFinalVoice	Ident(voice)	*Voice	*IntervocalicVoiceless
[tad]	*!		*	
☞[tat]		*		
UR: /tad-e/				
☞[tade]			*	
[tate]		*!		*

Table 5 Testing Hypothesis B with grammar (24)

UR: /tat/	*SyllableFinalVoice	Ident(voice)	*Voice	*IntervocalicVoiceless
[tad]	*!		*	
☞[tat]				
UR: /tat-e/				
[tade]		*!	*	
☞ *[tate]				*

In this simple example, the initial constraint ranking gleaned from the phonotactics did not have to be revised, but more realistic cases will involve multiple faithfulness constraints that cannot be ranked with respect to each other based on phonotactics alone. As a result, the initial ranking may fail to generate all of the mappings for the hypothesized URs. In such a case, the mismatches between the observed winners and the optimums can again be used by BCD to revise the initial ranking, with the revision that succeeds being the indicator of which hypothesized UR is correct. The interdependence problem thus points to its own solution, as inconsistencies in grammar–lexicon combinations provide the cues to revise both in an error-driven feedback loop.

The utility of assuming that if a form x is grammatical then so must be the mapping $x \rightarrow x$ is explored further in Tesar's (2014, 2017) subsequent work on *output-driven maps*.[14] The designation of a map as output-driven refers to the following entailment relation: "for every grammatical candidate A→X of the map, if candidate B→X has greater similarity than A→X, then B→X is also grammatical (it is part of the map)" (Tesar 2017: 150). Similarity here refers to the number of disparities (i.e., feature changes) between inputs and outputs. For example, páká → paká: has two disparities (one stress, one length) and paká → paká: has one (length only). *If* the map is output-driven, then the inclusion of páká → paká: implies the inclusion of the more similar paká → paká:.

Tesar's thesis is that the property of being output-driven imposes structure on the learner's hypothesis space that can be exploited during its search for the correct grammar and lexicon. Importantly, output-drivenness is a property of the map itself, not of the OT grammar that generates it (see Section 7 for more on this idea). This is what is meant by structuring the hypothesis space. The set of maps that can be generated by OT grammars is large – on account of its combinatorics ($k!$ possible rankings of k constraints, though more than one ranking may generate the same map) as well as its formal generative capacity (more on this in Section 3.3.1). The learner's assumption that its target grammar can only generate a subset of those maps eliminates a great many hypotheses.

As in Tesar and Prince (2007), the output-driven learner (ODL) undergoes a stage of phonotactic learning without any morphological awareness before receiving information about alternations in order to identify URs. At this stage, the entailment relation inherent to the output-driven property serves to eliminate entire sets of possible URs all at once. To see how, consider an observed SR like [paká:]. The learner constructs a hypothesis UR with only one disparity relative to that SR, such as /paká/. If BCD then concludes that the

---

[14] The term *map* here and elsewhere refers to the set of input–output string pairs generated by a grammar (i.e., it refers to the grammar's *extension*).

mapping of /paká/ → [paká:] is inconsistent, the learner can reject the hypothesis of /paká/ as well as any other UR hypotheses that are less similar to the SR than /paká/ is (e.g., /pa:ká/, /paka/, /páka/, etc.).

From there, the learner can conclude that any feature value shared by all remaining hypothesized URs must be present in the correct UR. Once an underlying feature value is set in this way, SRs in which that feature surfaces unfaithfully can provide further information about the correct ranking. For example, if [páka] is an SR and the [ka] morpheme has already been identified as having the UR /ka:/, then the constructed mapping /páka:/ → [páka] must be grammatical, because any other possibility will involve more disparities. This mapping can then be used to construct winner–loser pairs and adjust the constraint ranking if needed.

The use of inconsistency detection to identify environments in which a feature is contrastive has precedent in the contrast pair and ranking (CPR) information algorithm of Merchant (2008) and Merchant and Tesar (2008). Contrast pair and ranking has the advantage of being able to set multiple features at once by constructing *local lexica* for all possible settings of unset features, but the ODL is ultimately more efficient given that the number of lexica can grow quite large depending on how many features alternate.[15]

Looking beyond categorical grammars, the promise of probabilistic models for handling gradient phonotactics (see Section 4) lead to their application to a wider range of phonological learning problems, including the simultaneous learning of grammars and lexicons. For example, Jarosz (2006a, 2006b) characterizes this problem in the framework of maximum likelihood learning of lexicons and grammars (MLG), in which each possible constraint ranking is assigned a probability and the conditional probability of a candidate (given a UR) is summed across all rankings for which it is the winner. Another probability distribution across possible URs provides the conditional probability of a UR given a morpheme. The learning problem is then a matter of identifying the parameters for these distributions that maximize the likelihood of the training data (= morphologically analyzed SRs and their frequencies). Enacting richness of the base, the set of possible URs is rich, though not fully unconstrained. It is generated from the SRs based on all possible feature variants that could generate one of the observed SRs of the morpheme in question, as well as all possible insertions and deletions that could be generated under some constraint ranking. The learning algorithm is expectation maximization: starting from uniform distributions, the parameters are iteratively adjusted until convergence (i.e., the change from the previous iteration is below some threshold).

---

[15] The original ODL can only handle feature disparities between URs and SRs, putting aside the possibility of insertions and deletions. Follow-up work by Nyman and Tesar (2019) addresses that gap using a "presence feature" that signals the presence or absence of a segment.

Jarosz (2009) further shows how MLG as a probabilistic learner subsumes the kinds of ranking biases enacted by the OT learners discussed previously in this Element. The resulting grammars are restrictive in the sense that likelihood will be maximized by a grammar that maps as much of the rich base to observed forms as possible (i.e., by not wasting probability mass on unobserved forms). This works out to ranking markedness over faithfulness without an explicitly encoded bias. Working instead with MaxEnt, O'Hara (2017) shows that an explicit mechanism is also not needed for a probabilistic learner to learn abstract URs (i.e., URs with a combination of features that never surface together in a single SR), as these fall out naturally when observed gaps in segment distributions are minimized.

Another approach to UR learning has been the use of constraints on the URs themselves (Zuraw 2000; Boersma 2001). Apoussidou (2007) makes use of these *lexical (or UR) constraints* in an online error-driven learner. Lexical constraints prohibit a particular meaning–form pairing in the lexicon; for example, Apoussidou proposes the constraint in (27) as part of the grammatical stress system of Modern Greek:[16]

(27)   *|θalas-| "sea": Do not connect the meaning "sea" to |θalas-|

Each candidate UR has its own constraint. Learning then proceeds through a recognition stage and a virtual production stage. Recognition involves an RIP-like process of mapping an SR to its optimum candidate (UR, SR, meaning) triplet. Virtual production checks which triplet the current grammar selects for that particular meaning. If the same candidate is selected in recognition and virtual production, no change is needed. Otherwise, the error signals a constraint reranking (via the GLA).

Lexical constraints prohibiting (or requiring) particular URs in a particular language clearly cannot be part of an innate and universal CON. Though no algorithm is given, Apoussidou (2007: 170) suggests they could instead be induced whenever a new meaning–form combination is encountered. Going further, Nelson (2019) provides a method for inducing lexical constraints that also addresses the related problem of morpheme segmentation. Given an SR and the unordered set of morphemes it contains, lexical constraints are induced based on all possible segmentations of that SR. For example, if the SR [abc] contains two morphemes (M_1 and M_2), the possible segmentations are [ab-c] and [a-bc], and so the needed lexical constraints include M_1=ab (i.e., M_1 must be [ab]), M_1=c, M_1=a, M_1=bc, etcetera.

---

[16] Vertical bars are used to signify underlying forms, to distinguish them from two other levels of representation: surface forms (e.g., /(θá.la)sa/) that contain unpronounced hidden structure and overt pronounced forms (e.g., [θálasa]).

As both of these solutions depend on the UR being one of the SRs (i.e., the *basic alternant* constraint; see Kenstowicz and Kisseberth 1979: 202), abstract URs that contain underspecified segments will present a challenge.[17] Pater et al. (2012) address this by allowing for different URs to be selected in different contexts (i.e., overspecification).[18] With the inclusion of the UR constraints, their MaxEnt grammar identifies the most likely (UR, SR) combination for a given meaning in a way that captures broader generalizations in the language while still allowing for non-alternating morphemes (e.g., the three-way voicing contrast in Turkish analyzed by Inkelas et al. 1997 as a case of underspecification).[19]

Lastly, the hidden structure learning problem has also been explored in the context of the intermediate representations of derivational theories such as stratal OT (Bermúdez-Otero 1999, 2003; Kiparsky 2000) and HS (McCarthy 2000). Staubs and Pater (2016) show how the order of operations in an HS derivation can be established through the constraint weights assigned by a MaxEnt learner tasked with maximizing the likelihood of the observed SRs. Following Eisenstat (2009), they take the probability of an SR to be the summed probability of the UR–SR mappings that could have generated it. Extending this to HS, the probability of an SR is the summed probability of the *derivations* that could have generated it. A derivation's probability is the joint probability of its steps, with the probability of a step being the SR's share in the distribution over the candidate set. The initial step makes use of UR constraints to identify the most likely UR for a given meaning. Following assumptions of HS, subsequent steps identify the most likely candidate among a set generated by applying a single operation (e.g., one added stress or segment). Nazarov (2016) and Nazarov and Pater (2017) extend this approach to stratal OT, in which a word-level grammar is followed by a phrase-level one in which the constraint ranking/weighting can potentially differ.

As the scope of the work in this section has made clear, constraint-based grammars have enabled great progress on a variety of learning challenges, including noisy data and hidden structure. Following the theoretical assumption that the constraint set CON is innate and universal, the learners discussed previously in this Element are all in practice provided with the constraints

---

[17] Recent work by Wang and Hayes (2022) systematically explores the learning challenge of abstract URs by generating UR candidates for an EM-MaxEnt learner at different levels of the UR abstractness hierarchy discussed by Kenstowicz and Kisseberth (1977).

[18] The lexical constraints are still provided to their learner, but the possible URs are generated in a manner similar to Jarosz (2006a, 2006b). See also Eisenstat (2009).

[19] For an alternative approach to learning underspecification, see Belth (2023) for a modular learner that constructs a lexicon in an online fashion using the tolerance principle (Yang 2016) as a cue for when to abstract an underspecified UR from the observed surface variants.

relevant to the patterns in question. The work reviewed in the next section considers the alternative possibility that the constraints themselves are also learned, creating the potential for future work to integrate such a step into methods for grammar and lexicon learning.

3.2.3 Learning Constraints

Ellison (1991, 1992) describes an MDL approach to learning the inviolable constraints on a language's representations assumed by work in declarative phonology. As discussed in Section 2 in the context of learning rule-based grammars, MDL assesses a hypothesized grammar in terms of the size of the grammar itself as well as the encoding of the data with respect to that grammar, with the goal of minimizing that combined sum. A constraint template is assumed so that the cost of the template can be levied once regardless of how many constraints instantiate it. Constraints are selected iteratively, such that the value of adding each constraint can be assessed in comparison to a version of the grammar that lacks it. The search for constraints is terminated when the grammar can no longer be improved, meaning the cost of adding another constraint is not sufficiently balanced by a reduction in the cost of encoding the data.

Turning now to the learning of violable constraints, the highly influential MaxEnt phonotactic learner of Hayes and Wilson (2008) learns both the constraint weights and the constraints themselves. As with the MDL learner just described, the MaxEnt learner works from a constraint template in the form of a sequence of feature matrices bounded by a specified length. Constraints are selected from this hypothesis space using the heuristics of accuracy and generality. A constraint's *accuracy* is defined as an observed/expected (O/E) ratio of violations in the data under the currently hypothesized grammar. *Generality* means priority is given to constraints that are shorter and that include larger natural classes. The current constraint set is reweighted with each new constraint addition, and the search terminates when no constraints are left that are sufficiently accurate (or when a grammar of a designated size has been found).[20]

As a phonotactic model, MaxEnt interprets well-formedness as a probability distribution over all possible SRs. Since the focus is only on SRs, a candidate's probability is not conditioned on a particular UR, and faithfulness constraints play no role (i.e., only markedness constraints are learned). An individual SR's probability represents its share of the total *maxent values* (= *e* raised to the negation of the harmony score defined previously in Section 3.1) of all possible SRs. The learning objective is then to find the weights that maximize the

---

[20] For an alternative approach that conceives of the phonotactic grammar as a generative process instead of a set of constraints, see Linzen and O'Donnell (2015) and Futrell et al. (2017).

probability of the observed forms and minimize the probability of unobserved ones. Modifications and extensions of this approach have been applied to a range of phonological learning problems, including learning the features as well as the constraints (Nazarov 2016), distinguishing between true constraints and accidental gaps (Wilson and Gallagher 2018), the learning of nonlocal constraints (Gouskova and Gallagher 2020), the potential for a naturalness bias to rule out "accidentally true" constraints that hold without exception in the data but are not part of the speakers' grammatical knowledge (Hayes and White 2013), and the use of n-gram probabilities as a way of reducing the size of the hypothesis space of constraints (Nelson 2022).

3.3 Theory Comparison

To wrap up the discussion of constraint-based theories of phonology, this section turns to the use of computational and quantitative methods for theory comparison, including the comparison between rule- and constraint-based theories as well as comparisons among different constraint-based theories. These comparisons have been made using a variety of considerations, including formal complexity, learnability and convergence results, and expressivity with respect to questions of long-standing theoretical interest. In what follows, these will each be discussed in turn.

3.3.1 Complexity

The most common criteria by which rule- and constraint-based grammatical formalisms have been compared to each other include empirical adequacy, explanatory redundancy, and potential for corresponding learning algorithms, but computational complexity has also played a role. Within computational phonology, the well-known result that SPE grammars are regular relations provided the rules do not reapply to their own structural changes (Johnson 1972; Kaplan and Kay 1994) leads to the inevitable question of whether OT grammars preserve that property.[21] In short, the answer is no, but a line of work exploring different ways of implementing OT with finite-state machinery provided further insight into the sources of that increased power.

Gerdemann and Hulden (2012) provide a simple proof that OT is capable of generating non-regular relations, using the example grammar shown in Table 6. In the first tableau, the input /aaabb/ violates *ab and is mapped to the optimum

---

[21] Kaplan and Kay (1994) establish this result using one-way FSTs, which are strictly less expressive than two-way FSTs that can reread portions of the string. To reflect this distinction in expressivity, the class of mappings Kaplan and Kay studied is sometimes instead called the *rational* relations, with *regular* being reserved for the class generated by two-way FSTs (see Filiot and Reynier 2016).

Table 6 Counterexample to optimality theory being regular. Adapted from Gerdemann and Hulden (2012)

UR: /aaabb/	*ab	MAX
[aaabb]	*!	
☞[aaa]		**
[bb]		**!*

UR: /aabbb/	*ab	MAX
[aabbb]	*!	
[aa]		**!*
☞[bbb]		**

[aaa] in which both /b/'s are deleted. (For simplicity, DEP and Ident are not shown, but these are assumed to be ranked above *ab such that candidates like [aaacc] or [aaacbb] are also ruled out.) In the second tableau, the input /aabbb/ is instead mapped to [bbb], in which the two /a/'s are deleted.

More generally, inputs of the form $a^n b^m$ will always be mapped by this grammar to either a^n or b^m depending on which is larger: n or m. When deletion is the preferred repair for violations of *ab, optimization will insist on deleting as few segments as possible. The relation generated by this grammar ($a^n b^m \rightarrow a^n$ if $m < n$ and $a^n b^m \rightarrow b^m$ if $n < m$) is not finite-state describable.[22]

A finite-state version of OT then must impose certain restrictions to ensure the generated relations stay within the bounds of regular. For example, Ellison's (1994) implementation assumes (1) constraints are binary and regular (i.e., can be represented with an FST that maps candidates to their lists of marks), and (2) the candidate set produced by GEN is a regular language. Frank and Satta (1998) show that an upper bound on constraint violations – after which the grammar cannot make distinctions among candidates – suffices to make OT finite-state describable. However, Riggle (2004) is able to relax some of these restrictions by focusing on the set of contenders, or candidates that are not harmonically bounded, and using a monolithic evaluator instead of a cascade-style combination of individual constraints.[23] Next, comparing finite-state implementations of a parametrized metrical grid theory and an OT one (using

---

[22] See also Hao (2019) for a comparable result for HS.

[23] See Riggle (2004) and Chandlee and Jardine (2022) for more detailed discussions of the finite-state OT literature.

Karttunen's 1998 lenient composition operator to combine the constraints), Idsardi (2009) shows that the latter is far less efficient, requiring forty-five states compared to the two states required by the "rule-based" machine. And in more recent work, Lamont (2021) shows that OT can generate context-sensitive languages with constraints banning subsequences, and Lamont (2022) shows that even with simple constraints, OT can actually generate non-pushdown functions.

The regular/non-regular divide is particularly relevant for finite-state approaches, but the generation problem in OT has been a subject of broader concern. Eisner (2000) proves that OT is NP-hard by transforming the generation problem into the directed Hamiltonian graph problem, which is itself NP-complete. The proof assumes an OT-variant called Primitive OT (Eisner 1997), in which constraints dictate the extent to which constituents can overlap on an autoseg-mental-like timeline, but Idsardi (2006) shows that the same result holds assuming the more standard MAX, DEP, unigram and bigram markedness constraints, and *self-conjoined* constraints of the sort proposed by Ito and Meester (2003) to handle co-occurrence restrictions (though see Heinz et al. 2009 and Kornai 2009 for critical responses). More recently, Hao (2024) shows that the universal generation problem in OT (i.e., generation when CON is not fixed but provided as an input) is PSPACE-complete.

As results such as these make clear, the complexity of OT depends on what, if any, restrictions are assumed for the interacting components of GEN, EVAL, and CON. With respect to CON in particular, one approach to formalizing such restrictions has been the use of a constraint definition language (CDL) that specifies the syntactic primitives and rules of combination for constraints, as well as the means by which they calculate violation marks (see de Lacy 2011 for more discussion of CDLs). For example, Potts and Pullum (2002) use model theory to make the meaning of OT constraints more precise, in particular by characterizing candidates as a class of structures and defining a description logic for the constraints over that class (more will be said about model theory in Section 7.3). They show that a wide range of constraints can be thus described using a limited modal logic, while certain constraints types (e.g., output–output identity and inter-candidate sympathy) cannot (see Riggle 2004 and Jardine and Heinz 2016b for additional examples of CDLs). Given how much progress in OT has been driven by proposed additions to CON, CDLs offer a valuable means of studying the computational consequences of such proposals.

3.3.2 Learnability

This section touches on how learning and learnability have been used to compare constraint-based theories. For more comprehensive surveys of these topics, readers are referred to Tesar (2007), Heinz and Riggle (2011), Albright and Hayes (2014), Tessier (2017), Jarosz (2019), and Heinz and Rawski (2022).

Complexity results of the sort discussed in the previous section have also been established for various learning problems. But Magri (2013a) argues that the relevance of intractability results (which are not unique to OT) is less about choosing among grammatical formalisms and more about their implications for child language acquisition. For example, the strong consistency problem (i.e., finding a grammar that is consistent with most of the data) in OT is intractable, because the cyclic ordering problem (shown by Galil and Megiddo 1977 to be NP-complete) can be reduced to it. The weak version, in which the algorithm only needs to detect inconsistency without returning a grammar, is tractable (Tesar and Smolensky 2000), but as discussed previously (Sections 2 and 3.2.1), the phonological learner also needs to be concerned with the grammar's restrictiveness on account of the subset problem. Magri shows that even when assuming consistent data, the subset problem in OT (i.e., minimize r-measure) is also intractable.

The implications of these results are as follows. Despite the common assumption that CON is innate and universal, constraint demotion algorithms assume an arbitrary constraint set and therefore only make use of the logic of ranking and optimization itself. That logic is sufficient for the weak consistency problem, but the subset problem demands more, and this is true for both batch learners and error-driven online ones. As the latter type are a better model of acquisition stages, Magri conjectures that their limitations with respect to finding restrictive grammars may be overcome by making use of the added structure that distinguishes linguistically plausible rankings (defined, e.g., in terms of particular feature interactions).[24]

With respect to modeling acquisition, Magri (2012) also argues that both constraint demotion and *promotion* are desirable, if not necessary to capture acquisition trajectories (e.g., the use of different repair strategies over time). The GLA performs both of these operations, but it is not convergent in the general case (Pater 2008). Magri (2012) shows that the issue is the balance of promotion and demotion; the latter is needed to guarantee convergence, and so the former cannot overwhelm its effects. A solution exists, however, in the form of calibrating the amount p that winner-preferring constraints are promoted

---

[24] This assumed interdependence of the learning mechanism and the patterns being learned is also a theme of the learning research grounded in formal language theory, to which we will turn in Section 7.

such that it satisfies the formula in (28), where l is the number of un-dominated loser-preferring constraints and w is the number of winner-preferring constraints. Loser-preferring constraints are all demoted by a fixed amount.

(28) $p < \dfrac{l}{w}$

Magri argues that the resulting proof of efficient convergence means the GLA's lack of convergence cannot be used as evidence in favor of (MaxEnt-)HG – for which error-driven learners have also been proposed (Jäger 2007; Jesney and Tessier 2009; Tessier 2009; Boersma and Pater 2016, but see also Magri 2016) – though the desirability of promotion is itself an argument for numerical ranking, a requirement for the calibration solution. Magri (2013b) further shows that any instance of the OT ranking problem can be solved by converting it into an instance of the HG weighting problem, countering previous arguments that HG's affinity for machine learning algorithms is evidence of its computational superiority over OT. As a demonstration, he shows how the GLA revised with the calibrated promotion amount can be reinterpreted as the perceptron algorithm used to find the weight vectors in HG.

Nonetheless, arguments about convergence and online learning are not the only consideration in the debate over weighted versus ranked constraints. The next section will turn to questions of expressivity, particularly with respect to the handling of gradience, variation, and exceptions.

3.3.3 Expressivity

Constraint-based phonotactic models have served as a proving ground for well-known phonological principles such as the sonority sequencing principle (see Daland et al. 2011) and the obligatory contour principle (OCP) (Leben 1973). The latter in particular has received a lot of attention in model comparison studies exploring different options for the source of gradient well-formedness. Frisch et al. (2004) propose that the co-occurrence restrictions on consonants in Arabic roots (Greenberg 1950) are best explained with a gradient version of the OCP, for which the probability of a violation is a function of the consonants' similarity. Gradient constraints reflect speakers' knowledge of which patterns are over- and underrepresented in their lexicons, quantified as the ratio of the number of observed (O) consonant pairs to the number of pairs that would be expected (E) if consonants combined freely. In their analysis of Arabic, they show that O/E ratios decrease as similarity increases, a level of detail missed by categorical constraints.

They define the similarity of two consonants in terms of shared natural classes. The effect of subsidiary features (i.e., non-place features that influence the strength of the OCP–place effect) is then determined by the language's inventory. But Coetzee and Pater (2008) argue that this is too restrictive and cannot account for the role of subsidiary features in the OCP effects in Muna (Austronesian). Their own approach, situated in HG, instead allows for the relevant subsidiary features to be identified for each place by providing constraints for all possible place/subsidiary feature combinations. Taking a different tack, Anttila (2008) demonstrates that categorical ranked constraints can account for gradience by relating well-formedness to complexity, with complexity defined in terms of how many constraints need to be ranked below faithfulness for a form to surface faithfully. This leads to the complexity hypothesis, which states that O/E is inversely correlated with grammatical complexity: the more complex a structure is, the more underrepresented it will be. In addition to modeling gradience with a categorical grammar, this approach offers clear typological predictions for quantitative patterns: those that obtain regardless of how the constraints are ranked are predicted to be universal, with language-specific variation limited to complexity orderings that depend on the constraint ranking.

This cluster of studies demonstrates the use of O/E values as a test for how well a model's predictions align with reality. However, Wilson and Obdeyn (2009) argue that O/E is not a statistically sound estimate of the OCP's effects, because it does not account for the interaction of other constraints that might affect the observed frequency of a consonant pair (e.g., positional constraints for the individual members of the pair). Rather than attempting to isolate the effect of a single constraint, competing models should be assessed based on their fit to the data in its entirety. At the same time, just searching for the model that best fits the data can lead to the selection of a model that is more complex and therefore less restrictive as far as the limits it places on cross-linguistic variation. They advocate instead for prioritizing restrictiveness even at the cost of fit – for example, by using the Laplace approximation to combine the measures of data fit and model complexity.

They use this technique to compare MaxEnt grammars with the different versions of OCP–place discussed previously in this Element – namely Frisch et al.'s (2004) similarity and Coetzee and Pater's (2008) acceptability – with their own proposed version that employs language-specific weighted features in which the similarity of two sounds is the sum of the weights of their shared features. Apparent differences in the effect of subsidiary features are explained by the different weights on place features, not as interactions of these feature types. If it appears that subsidiary features contribute differently across places, it is because their influence will be more prominent with low-weighted place features but masked with high-weighted ones. Their weighted features model outperforms the others on the same test cases from Arabic and Muna.

Another prominent argument in favor of weighted constraints is their ability to model the cumulative effects of violating multiple markedness constraints, in contrast to ranked constraint grammars in which only the highest-ranking decisive constraint violation matters (see Pater 2009). Because of cumulativity, it is possible for multiple violations of lower-weighted constraints to have a greater effect than more highly weighted ones. It is also possible for single violations of multiple lower-weighted constraints to "gang up" and have more influence than a single more highly weighted constraint. In HG, the harmony of a candidate that violates multiple markedness constraints reflects additive (or linear) cumulativity compared to a candidate that violates only one of them. But this is not necessarily the desired result. In artificial grammar learning (AGL) experiments, Breiss (2020), Durvasula and Liter (2020), and Breiss and Albright (2022) all found evidence that cumulative markedness is *greater* than the sum of its parts: forms that violate multiple constraints appear to be subject to an added penalty over and above the contributions of the individual constraints.

To test different theories' ability to capture this effect of *superlinearity*, Smith and Pater (2020) compare the performance of stochastic OT, noisy HG, and MaxEnt grammars with the variation of schwa deletion in French. The likelihood of a schwa deleting is conditioned by two contextual factors: whether the following syllable is stressed and whether the schwa follows one or two consonants. They compared the models' fit on experimental data in which participants indicated whether they would pronounce a schwa in various phonological contexts and found that MaxEnt and noisy HG had the greatest success due to their ability to accommodate superlinearity. Breiss and Albright (2022) also found that their experimental results were compatible with a MaxEnt grammar under certain weighting conditions, and further that the strength of the superlinearity effect of two constraints depends on the strength of their restrictions (i.e., how many exceptions are present in the training data).

How to handle lexical exceptions to otherwise productive patterns has itself been a prominent question of interest. It has been shown that stochastic OT's ranking mechanism allows for a grammatical solution via dually listing morphologically complex forms that vacillate and singly listing those that do not (Zuraw 2000; Hayes and Londe 2006). For non-derived forms, however, Moore-Cantwell and Pater (2016) propose a MaxEnt grammar that includes constraints indexed to particular lexical items. Shih and Inkelas (2016) also call on MaxEnt to model lexically conditioned variation in Mende (Mande; Sierra Leone) tonotactics, in which the relative frequency of different tone melodies depends on part of speech. Their multilevel model includes a base grammar that predicts the overall distribution of tone patterns adjusted by a set of word class-specific weights for the same set of constraints. Similarly, Zymet (2018, 2019) argues that as a single-level regression model, MaxEnt struggles to balance the contributions of grammatical and lexical constraints by treating them as equally likely sources of explanation for the statistical patterns in the data. In contrast, hierarchical regression's nesting structure allows the grammar's contribution to be prioritized by modeling general constraints as fixed effects and lexical constraints as random effects. The overall rate at which a generalization holds across the lexicon is captured as the fixed effect, with random effects accounting for lexically specific deviations from that rate.

As much of the work reviewed in this section makes clear, capturing non-categorical aspects of phonological knowledge has been an area of great interest. The next section focuses on one particular type of knowledge – phonotactics – and the various ways lexical statistics and other sources of information have been used to account for the observed gradience in acceptability judgments.

4 Gradient Acceptability and Lexical Statistics

It has long been recognized that speakers have knowledge of which sound sequences are and are not possible in their languages (i.e., phonotactic knowledge). A classic example is *blick* versus **bnick*; neither is an actual word of English, but speakers reliably recognize that only the former is a *possible* word (Chomsky and Halle 1965). Put another way, *blick* is treated as an accidental gap in the lexicon, whereas **bnick* is prohibited from the lexicon due to some type of grammatical constraint. The observed contrast between pairs like *blick* / **bnick* suggests a categorical model in which words are either allowed or disallowed based on their particular sequencing of sounds, and the presence of a single disallowed sequence is enough to condemn the entire word. Indeed *blick* and *bnick* are nearly identical, so they cannot be bad across the board. Rather, the problem with **bnick* is isolated to a subword component, namely the sequence #bn.[25]

Coleman (1996) tested the psychological reality of such constraints by collecting acceptability judgments from English speakers for matched nonce words with and without a phonotactic violation (e.g., **mlisless* versus *glisless*). The task was categorical (e.g., forced choice response to whether the word is or could be a word of English), and a word's overall rating was calculated as the proportion of participants who accepted it. Contrary to the predictions of the

---

[25] Following the conventions of SPE, # is used to mark the word boundary.

categorical model, the results indicated that a single disallowed subword component does not in fact make the word completely unacceptable. In addition, words that did not violate any constraints but were made up of low-frequency components were rated lower than words with high-frequency components, despite both word types being fully grammatical.

This effect of frequency is taken as evidence that speakers are not just aware of what is and is not possible, but can draw on more detailed knowledge of distributional patterns to assess the *gradient acceptability* of actual and novel words. But this in turn raises the question of which lexical statistics best account for this knowledge (i.e., what frequencies are speakers attuned to). A baseline approach defines *phonotactic probability* with an *n*-gram model in which probabilities are assigned to sequences of length *n* based on their frequency in a training corpus. For example, in a bigram model ($n = 2$), the probability of the sequence *bl* is calculated as in (29),

$$(29) \qquad P(bl) = \frac{C(bl)}{C(b)}$$

where *C(bl)* is the number of times *bl* appears in the corpus and *C(b)* is the number of times *b* appears (i.e., the *unigram* count of *b*).[26] The probability of an entire word is the product of the probabilities of its component bigrams. The difference in acceptability between *blick* and **bnick* then would be accounted for if $P(bl) > P(bn)$ according to a corpus of English.

This baseline model, however, fails to capture the fact that *bn* as a sequence is not itself problematic (e.g., **subnet, abnormal, abnegate**). It is only a problem in a particular position, namely the beginning of the word. One way to address this flaw would be with a *trigram* model, in which case we would expect $P(\#bl) > P(\#bn)$.[27] But Vitevitch et al. (1997) go further to assess the role of position in phonotactic acceptability. They constructed nonce CVC syllables of high and low probability, with probability determined using both transition (i.e., bigram) probabilities and the probabilities of segments in particular positions (initial-medial-final). Bisyllabic forms were then created that varied in stress placement and covered all possible combinations of high- and low-probability syllables. Their task elicited gradience directly by asking participants to rate words on a scale from 1 (Good) to 10 (Bad). They found that stress placement as well as probability played a role in these

---

[26] More specifically, this is the *conditional* probability, $P(l \mid b)$, or the probability of seeing *l* given that you just saw *b*. The ratio of counts can be interpreted as: of all the times *something* followed *b*, how often was that something an *l*?

[27] Indeed we would expect $P(\#bn) = 0$, given the absence of English words that start with *bn*, but the use of smoothing techniques to assign nonzero probabilities to all sequences is common (see Jurafsky and Martin 2008).

judgments: words with first-syllable stress were rated higher than forms with second-syllable stress, and words with two high- (low-) probability syllables were rated highest (lowest) overall.

Similarly, the probabilistic parser of Coleman and Pierrehumbert (1997) incorporates the role of prosodic structure via a (non-recursive) context-free grammar in which the non-terminals encode stress, syllable, and positional information. In the example rule in (30), S, O, and R represent syllable, onset, and rhyme, respectively, and the "sf" designation further indicates that these components are stressed and final.

(30)   Ssf → Osf Rsf

Each word component is assigned a path based on the rules that generate it, and the probability of a path is computed from a parsed training corpus. The probability of an entire word is then the product of its component paths. While the probability of a word's worst component was found to be significantly correlated with the experimental results of Coleman (1996), the strongest predictor was the log probability of the entire word (with log probabilities being used to address the effect of word length). In this global and probabilistic approach to word acceptability, the presence of well-formed subword components can mitigate the effect of unattested or infrequent ones.

Another whole-word conception of likelihood is in terms of overall similarity to the existing words in the lexicon. Greenberg and Jenkins (1964) define this similarity in terms of the number of substitutions needed to convert a nonword into an actual word, and Ohala and Ohala (1986) provide experimental evidence that English speakers are in fact sensitive to varying degrees of similarity among nonwords.[28] This conception of a word's similarity has been extended to define its *neighborhood density*, or the number of existing words it is similar to. For example, *blick* is one substitution away from a number of existing words such as *brick, black, block, slick, click, flick, blip*, etcetera. How similar an existing word has to be to count as a "neighbor" can vary, but a common definition is that it requires a single string edit operation, to include additions and deletions as well as substitutions.

Of course, phonotactic probability and neighborhood density are correlated – forms with low- (high-) probability subword components will also have small (large) neighborhoods – making it difficult to tease apart which one is responsible for speakers' acceptability ratings. The study of Bailey and Hahn (2001), however, aimed to do exactly that. Moving beyond the "single string edit" definition

---

[28] See also Keane et al. (2017) for a comparison of mathematical approaches to characterizing hand shape similarity in sign languages.

of a neighbor, they instead propose a more sophisticated generalized neighbor-hood model, in which edit operations are weighted to reflect the phonological distance between two forms (e.g., *back* differs from both *pack* and *sack* by one substitution, but the difference between /b/ and /p/ is smaller than the difference between /b/ and /s/ in terms of shared features). They found that both phonotactic probability and lexical neighborhoods have significant effects on acceptability, and that one is not subsumed by the other. However, given that less than half of the variance in their collected ratings was accounted for with these measures combined, they ultimately conclude that there is still more to understand about these factors in particular and gradient acceptability in general.

When teasing apart the relative influences of phonotactic probability and neighborhood density, Shademan (2006) argues for a need to consider task effects. In particular, the inclusion of actual words in the set of experimental stimuli (as in Bailey and Hahn 2001) may amplify lexical effects, as was previously suggested by Vitevitch and Luce (1998) in the context of word-processing tasks. Shademan's own experiments tested words in the four logic-ally possible combinations of high/low probability and high/low lexical similarity. When only nonce words were included, probability had a greater correlation with the acceptability ratings (scored from 1 to 7) than lexical similarity. When both actual and nonce words were included, the effect of lexical similarity became more pronounced, though it still was not as strong as the effect of probability.

Even with their relative roles still in question, phonotactic probability and neighborhood density do not tell the whole story of gradient acceptability. Other work has identified significant contributions of phonological knowledge beyond prosodic structure. Hay et al. (2004) tested nonce words containing nasal-obstruent clusters that vary in their frequency (e.g., [nt] is very frequent, [mθ] is unattested, and [nf] is attested but infrequent). Cluster frequency was highly correlated with participants' acceptability ratings (which were determined on a scale of 1 to 10), at least for the attested clusters. The unattested clusters unexpectedly defied this pattern, being rated higher than some low-probability attested clusters. A follow-up experiment suggested that the additional information speakers might be incorp-orating into their assessment of nonce word likelihood includes morphological analysis (i.e., parsing unattested clusters as spanning a morpheme boundary) as well as long-distance phonological effects like the OCP.

Another potentially valuable source of information missed by basic *n*-gram models is the feature-based representations of segments, as in the Hayes and Wilson (2008) phonotactic model (discussed previously in Section 3.2.3). To further explore this potential, Albright (2009) uses the probability of sequences of natural classes in addition to specific segments to estimate the likelihood of an onset cluster that is not present in a training corpus. For example, both [bd] and [bn] are unattested onsets in English, which would be treated similarly by a bigram model. By generalizing over features instead, Albright's model predicts the preference for [bn] because it has more features in common with attested onsets compared to [bd].

Yet another line of research has instead questioned the initial assumption that gradient acceptability ratings reflect gradient grammatical knowledge. In addition to the explanatory power of phonotactic probability and neighborhood density not being complete, Gorman (2013) shows that it is not even consistent, as in some cases these gradient models are outperformed by a baseline categorical model that only considers whether a word includes an illicit component. Like Shademan (2006), Gorman suggests the potential for task effects to play a role in gradient acceptability, including the implications of asking participants to use a scale in the first place (e.g., Armstrong et al. 1983 show that when given the option to use intermediate ratings, participants will provide gradient judgments on how odd or even a number is, even though these properties are categorical by definition).

Kahng and Durvasula (2023) also directly challenge the assumption that gradient acceptability reflects an underlying grammar of gradient generalizations, arguing that the perceptual system introduces bias and variance that can influence the cline of acceptability. In their experiment, Korean speakers rated forms with illicit clusters lower than those in which a vowel breaks up the cluster. More surprising, clusters with [c] as the first consonant were rated higher than those with [b] as the first consonant, even though both clusters are unattested. This discrepancy is hard to explain as a gradient generalization. A feature-based approach would actually predict [bC] to be better than [cC], since the former has more features in common with attested sequences (i.e., nasal clusters are attested, so the voicing of [b] should give it an advantage).

In addition to rating acceptability, participants were also asked to identify the medial vowel in the stimuli (with "no vowel" as an option). Factoring that information into the analysis, the authors found that (1) participants rated forms more acceptable when they heard an illusory vowel in the disallowed clusters, and (2) they were more likely to hear illusory vowels in [cC] compared to [bC]. Based on this, they propose a model in which categorical grammatical constraints operate over a probability distribution of perceptual representations. Hearing an illusory vowel in illicit forms results in a perceived *licit* form that the grammar recognizes as well formed, with the likelihood of hearing these vowels (i.e., the source of gradience) attributed to the perceptual system. They conclude with a larger suggestion that proposals for gradient grammatical generalizations based on acceptability judgments should be supported by an investigation into what participants actually perceived.[29]

How best to account for phonotactic knowledge remains an ongoing question of interest. We will return to research on phonotactics – particularly how they are learned – in Section 7.1. But first, the next two sections will briefly survey the past and current phonological research employing information theory and neural networks, respectively.

5 Information Theory

This section demonstrates the utility and flexibility of information theoretic methods by highlighting examples of their application to a range of problems of phonological interest.[30]

5.1 Features and Natural Classes

A great deal of work on phonological learning assumes – out of either principle or convenience – an innate feature set that can be used to define natural classes of sounds, but distributional data has also been used to induce those classes directly. The four-step method proposed by Mayer (2020) makes use of vector embeddings of sounds that represent the important aspects of their distribution, such as counts of all trigrams that include the target sound (normalized using positive pointwise mutual information, or PPMI). Phonological classes are then identified using principal component analysis (PCA) to reduce dimensionality, followed by k-means clustering over each principal component. Because the number of clusters is not known in advance, the Bayesian information criterion (BIC) (Schwarz 1978) is used to find the value of k that best balances model complexity (= number of clusters) and fit (= distance from the cluster centroids). Principal component analysis and clustering are performed recursively on discovered classes until the latter only identifies a single cluster.[31]

5.2 Allophones and Neutralization

Peperkamp et al. (2006) use the Kullback–Leibler divergence metric to compare the distributions of pairs of segments, taking a high value to indicate an allophonic relationship. Which of the pair is the allophone is determined using relative entropy, assuming the allophone will have higher entropy than

---

[29] See also Hale and Reiss (2008: chapter 5) for arguments that gradient acceptability should be attributed to performance factors and is not the responsibility of the grammar.

[30] See also Coleman (2014) for more context on the role of information theory in early generative phonology.

[31] The further problem of inducing features from the discovered classes is taken up by Mayer and Daland (2020).

the phoneme. To incorporate phonological knowledge, such as the fact that allophones tend to be similar to their phonemes, as well as the contexts they appear in, they add linguistic filters to weed out pairs of segments that happen to meet their selection criteria but lack these relationships. One clue is if a third segment exists that is intermediate between the two. Another is if the allophone is more distant from its context than the phoneme from which it is derived. The need for these filters means that distributional information alone is insufficient to detect true allophonic relationships; prior knowledge about which pairs of sounds *might* be allophones is also needed. Calamaro and Jarosz (2015) extend this model to learn cases of neutralization, in which two sounds that otherwise contrast are complementary in a particular context (i.e., have partially overlapping distributions).

5.3 Phonotactics and Phonological Structure

Goldsmith and Riggle (2012) demonstrate the value of information theoretic methods for assessing the need for and contribution of phonological structure. The average positive log probability (i.e., entropy) of a dataset under a model tells us how surprising or accidental the data is according to that model. The difference in entropy between two models reveals the contribution (either positive or negative) of added structure. For example, a comparison of unigram (no structure) and bigram (linear structure) models can motivate something akin to bigram markedness constraints: absent a constraint against a sequence *ab*, the probability of that sequence is the product of the individual probabilities of *a* and *b* (i.e., these are independent events). But the probability of *ab* being greater or less than this joint probability signals an interaction between them (i.e., they are more or less likely to occur together than apart).

Using Finnish vowel harmony as an example, they show that a bigram model reduces entropy (i.e., assigns higher probability) compared to a unigram model, justifying its added structure. From there they conduct further comparisons with bigram models with more structure, such as simulating autosegmental tiers using bigrams over classes. Following Goldsmith and Xanthos's (2009) procedure for discovering phonological categories, they find the partition of Finnish segments into two categories (each a probability distribution over its segments) that maximizes the probability of the data (computed with a two-state hidden Markov model). The resulting partition separates the inventory into vowels and consonants. Repeating this process on just the vowels discovers the categories of front and back that are relevant to Finnish's vowel harmony patterns, with neutral vowels given close to equal emission probabilities from both states. With this model of the vowel tier, a word's probability is the product of the probability of its sequence of vowels and the bigram probability of the original string, in which all vowels are collapsed to the symbol V. Because the resulting cost of this model is actually higher than the unaugmented bigram model, the authors appeal to a Boltzmann model to combine unigram, bigram, and vowel-to-vowel probabilities. By capturing nonlocal vowel-to-vowel dependencies as well as less commonly recognized local consonant–vowel effects, their model provides a better fit than either the unigram or bigram models alone.

The broader contribution of this work is the use of information theoretic model comparison methods to justify the increased complexity of added structure rather than assuming its inclusion as a matter of course.[32] These methods also provide the opportunity to verify assumptions that theories otherwise make for us by default – for example, that a language with vowel harmony necessitates a tier-based representation in which consonants do not contribute information. Goldsmith and Riggle's (2012: 880) case study on Finnish reveals the "more complex linguistic reality" that even in the presence of vowel harmony, consonants may in fact condition the choice of a following vowel.

6 Neural Networks

The potential of connectionist models of morpho-phonology has long been recognized (e.g., Rumelhart and McClelland 1986; Gasser and Lee 1990), though perhaps underutilized, with current developments sparking renewed interest. Due to space limitations, this section will be necessarily brief, but readers are referred to Alderete and Tupper (2018) as well as any of the works cited in what follows for more context on and examples of the use of neural networks for phonological learning, modeling, and theorizing. Pater (2019) in particular provides an accessible introduction to neural networks and a valuable discussion of their history and potential for greater integration with generative linguistics research.[33] Taking an even stronger stance on the future, Boersma et al. (2020) argue that only a neural network model will be capable of accounting for the full range of behavioral data associated with the phonetics – phonology interface.

As articulated by Goldsmith (1992a), neural networks offer a means for conducting phonological analysis without committing to typical generative assumptions of a highly structured LAD, as well as a clearer route to drawing connections with other areas of cognitive science. As an example, Goldsmith

---

[32] As another example, Shih (2017) employs the Akaike information criterion (AIC) to justify the inclusion of local constraint conjunction in HG to accommodate superlinearity effects.

[33] See also the series of responses to Pater (2019) that appear in the same issue of *Language* (Volume 95 Number 1).

(1992b) presents a case study on using a neural network to model stress patterns. The units of the network correspond to the bottom row of a metrical grid (i.e., syllables), with stress corresponding to local maxima (greater activation than neighboring units). Activation may be inherent (determined by syllable position or weight) or derived by lateral inhibition of a neighboring unit. Particular settings of inherent activation and the inhibitory weights simulates effects like alternating stress and avoidance of stress clash. These effects are achieved through iterative recomputation until equilibrium, rather than through an ordered derivation that manipulates hidden structure. Goldsmith and Larson (1993) further show how syllabification can be modeled using activation to encode a segment's level of sonority, where a local maxima this time identifies a syllable's nucleus. Language-specific constraints or parameters are the result of different weights that control the spread of activation through the network, as well as activation thresholds that determine what counts as a peak.[34]

Given that the potential for these models to provide insight into language acquisition and cognition depends on their interpretability, several researchers have sought evidence of linguistic structure in the patterns of activation of hidden layers. For example, Alishahi et al. (2017) present results from experiments showing that phonemes can be recovered from the hidden layer representations of a recurrent neural network (RNN) trained to map pairs of spoken language and images into a semantic space. Success of phoneme recovery was greatest with the early (first and second) hidden layers and then decreased with each successive layer. Similarly, Smith et al. (2021) test a gestural harmony (Smith 2018) account of stepwise vowel harmony with an encoder–decoder model that maps strings of phonological units to sequences of articulator movements. The decoder's patterns of attention indicated that it was attentive to states corresponding to harmony-triggering vowels throughout the span of the word, consistent with the gestural overlap account of vowel harmony.

A clear advantage of neural networks for modeling acquisition is their ability to work with raw speech data directly, rather than the discrete input representations assumed by the majority of phonological learning models. This potential integration of phonetic and phonological learning is explored with a generative adversarial network (GAN) in Beguš (2020a, 2020b). Generative adversarial networks consist of a *generator* network tasked with generating data and a *discriminator* network tasked with determining whether an input is real or

---

[34] The use of activation values to encode variables like stress and sonority along with activation thresholds enables a combination of gradient and discrete representations, an idea explored further in the framework of gradient symbol processing (Smolensky and Legendre 2006; Smolensky et al. 2014) and gradient harmonic grammar (Smolensky and Goldrick 2016; Hsu 2022).

generated. The two networks are trained in tandem such that the discriminator's pattern of errors is used by the generator to improve its ability to generate data (i.e., its ability to fool the discriminator). Beguš (2020a, 2020b) used English data to train a GAN to generate voiceless stop-vowel sequences with and without an initial /s/. In the generated samples, the voice onset time (VOT) of the vowel was significantly shorter in the presence of the initial /s/, as predicted by the English pattern of allophonic variation between aspirated and unaspirated voiceless stops. To again address the question of interpretability and better understand the actual learning mechanisms at work, Beguš proposes a logistic regression–based method for finding correlations between the model's latent space and output variables such as presence versus absence of /s/.

In other work, neural networks are used to test the necessity of various types of linguistic structure for learning phonological patterns. For example, Doucette (2017) showed that phonotactic learning with an RNN is possible without relying on repeated features (i.e., alpha variables), and Mayer and Nelson's (2020) RNN phonotactic learner performed comparably to Hayes and Wilson's (2008) MaxEnt learner on Finnish vowel harmony, even without the augmentation of a tier. Prickett and Pater (2022) likewise forgo the need for prespecified constraints with an encoder–decoder model that achieved state-of-the-art accuracy on Tesar and Smolensky's (2000) stress pattern dataset and correctly generalized 112 of its 124 patterns. Delving further into learning biases, Prickett (2019) shows that learning in a sequence-to-sequence model can simulate proposed biases for learning process interactions, namely *maximal utilization* (all rules apply maximally; Kiparsky 1968) and *transparency* (interactions are not opaque; Kiparsky 1971). And Prickett (2021) argues that such models also capture formal language theoretic complexity biases of the sort discussed in the next section.

In addition to addressing the challenges of interpretability, future research using neural networks will hopefully shed light on how the choice of architecture and other design options affect what they can learn, as well as how these choices relate to the kinds of grammatical distinctions that linguists make. One approach to understanding neural networks has been to draw on tools from *formal language theory* (see Merrill 2023 for an overview), which we turn to in the next section.

7 Formal Language Theory (FLT)

A formal language theoretic approach to phonology emphasizes the formal structure of linguistic patterning in order to identify abstract universal properties, which in practice often relate to computational complexity. This formal structure is recognized by first representing phonological patterns with mathematical objects. For example, a phonotactic constraint like *[−son, +voice]# (i.e., words cannot end with voiced obstruents) can be represented with a set of strings that do not violate it (e.g., {*aba, ba, ap, pa, . . .*}) or a function that maps a given string to 0 or 1 depending on whether it violates the constraint (e.g., $f(aba) = 0, f(ab) = 1$, etc.).[35] Similarly, a phonological rule can be represented with a function (obligatory rule) or relation (optional rule) that maps an input to an output or set of outputs, respectively (e.g., $f(ab) = ap$ or {*ab, ap*}). The advantage of representing patterns in this way is the ability to identify their invariant structural properties (examples of which will be discussed in what follows), which hold regardless of the choice of grammatical formalism (rules, constraints, etc.).

Importantly, this emphasis on structure is fully compatible with statistical and quantitative approaches. For example, Hayes and Wilson's (2008) MaxEnt phonotactic learner (discussed in Section 3.2.3) makes use of a template for constraints in order to structure and narrow the hypothesis space. Formal language theory studies different kinds of templates, identifying what kinds of patterns they can and cannot express and what distinctions algorithms have to make to learn them. These results will be true regardless of whether or not the constraints are weighted or used to derive probability distributions.

Foundational work in this vein includes the aforementioned (Section 3.3.1) independent discovery by Johnson (1972) and Kaplan and Kay (1994) that SPE grammars are regular provided the rules do not reapply to their own structural changes.[36] This means an individual phonological rule can be compiled into an FST), and – since the regular relations are closed under composition – an ordered set of rules can likewise be represented with a single FST (i.e., the entire grammar is also regular). This finding established a computational boundary between phonology and other domains like morphology and syntax, which include patterns that are more complex than regular (see Carden 1983; Culy 1985; Shieber 1985; Kobele 2006; Heinz and Idsardi 2011, 2013). It also indicated that while SPE captures the basic intuition that phonological changes affect sounds in particular contexts, as a grammatical formalism, context-sensitive rules are more powerful than necessary for phonology.

---

[35] The co-domain of the function is {0, 1} under the assumption of a categorical phonotactic grammar. A gradient phonotactic grammar can also be modeled as a function with a real number co-domain. See Heinz and Riggle (2011) for more on how the categorical-versus-gradient distinction does not affect computational complexity in the sense that is relevant to FLT.

[36] The need for this restriction on application is illustrated with the example rule $\emptyset \rightarrow ab \, / \, a \underline{\quad} b$ (Kaplan and Kay 1994: 346). An "ab" string inserted by this rule could serve as the context for an additional insertion, in which case the rule generates the context-free language $a^n b^n$.

The finite-state modeling of phonology has also been a productive route to the development of software for implementing morpho-phonological systems (Beesley and Karttunen 2003; Hulden 2009; Aksёnova 2020; Gorman and Sproat 2021). Koskenniemi's (1983) two-level rule approach in particular has served as the basis for morphological analyzers for several languages, including low-resource languages that are less amenable to deep-learning approaches (e.g., Çöltekin 2010 and Washington et al. 2012).

Regularity then provides a well-defined proposed computational universal that is sufficiently expressive while ruling out a great many non-phonological patterns. However, Heinz (2011a, 2011b) – the culmination of a line of work initiated in Heinz (2007, 2009, 2010b) – offers the further hypothesis that phonological patterns are in fact *subregular* and belong to proper subsets of the regular languages and relations. This hypothesis is motivated by (1) typology, as the regular classes still admit phonologically implausible patterns; and (2) learnability, as the regular classes are not learnable under a variety of settings, including in the limit from positive data (Gold 1967) and the probably approximately correct framework (Valiant 1984, 2013).

With respect to typology, the subregular hypothesis offers clear and testable predictions designed to advance our understanding of the nature of phonological computation. For example, Gainor et al. (2012) and Heinz and Lai (2013) show that progressive and regressive vowel harmony is not just regular but subsequential (i.e., deterministic), and dominant-recessive and stem-controlled harmony patterns are what they call weakly deterministic.[37] In contrast, unattested patterns like Sour Grapes (Padgett 1995; Wilson 2003) and Majority Rules (Lombardi 1999; Baković 2000) fall outside of these boundaries (the latter is in fact non-regular). In the same vein, Jardine (2016a) argues that tonal patterns regularly exhibit greater computational complexity compared to segmental ones.

Such hypotheses are informed by the current state of knowledge of what is and is not attested, and therefore serve to highlight what kinds of patterns we should be looking for in order to extend that state of knowledge. In response to Heinz and Lai (2013) and Jardine (2016a), McCollum et al. (2020) and Meinhardt et al. (2024) present vowel harmony patterns that meet Jardine's (2016a) definition of *unbounded circumambience* (= the conditions for a change require unbounded lookahead in both directions from the target) and therefore serve as evidence that challenges his argument.[38] The latter work further draws a distinction between such patterns and those they call unbounded *semiambient*

---

[37] See Mohri (1997) for more on subsequential functions and their use in speech processing.

[38] Importantly, though, Jardine's (2016a) typological hypothesis is not a categorical one; indeed he also discusses Yaka vowel harmony as a counterexample.

(= the conditions for a change require unbounded lookahead in at most one direction from the target).[39] These kinds of typological investigations thus result in valuable, nuanced characterizations of the computations necessary to recognize or represent a phonological pattern.

With respect to learnability, the fact that the regular languages and relations are not learnable from positive data means the property of regularity does not sufficiently limit the hypothesis space of a phonological learner. In contrast, the subregular properties that delimit proper subsets of regular do enable learning under these conditions. The next two sections review the work demonstrating that potential in the learning of phonotactics and mappings, respectively, much of which builds on computational learning theory (Osherson et al. 1986; Jain et al. 1999; Mohri et al. 2018) and grammatical inference (de la Higuera 2010; Heinz and Sempere 2016; Wieczorek 2017).

7.1 Phonotactic Learning

Any phonotactic learner must assume something about the hypothesis space of possible constraints that it navigates. As noted previously, FLT-based approaches to phonotactic learning prioritize the nature of those assumptions by characterizing the formal structure of the patterns themselves. For example, focusing on stress patterns, Heinz (2007, 2009) formalizes phonological locality with a property called *neighborhood-distinctness*, defined in automata-theoretic terms as not containing multiple states that share the same set of incoming and outgoing paths of designated lengths (or locality windows). A survey of 109 stress patterns compiled by Bailey (1995) and Gordon (2002) – now available in the StressTyp2 database (Goedemans et al. 2015) – revealed that all of the patterns have this property. Furthermore, roughly 75 percent of them are strictly local (SL) (Edlefson et al. 2008; Rogers and Lambert 2019), which means they belong to a highly restrictive class of formal languages recognizable by devices that only track contiguous sub-strings of bounded length (McNaughton and Papert 1971; Rogers et al. 2010; Rogers and Pullum 2011). This length is often referred to as the language's k-value, so, for example, an SL language with $k=2$ can be represented with a grammar of banned 2-length substrings (called k-factors, or, in this case, 2-factors).[40]

---

[39] To distinguish these categories, Meinhardt et al. (2024) provide a formal definition of process interaction, a topic of broad interest in theoretical phonology. See also Baković and Blumenfeld (2019) for an algebraic treatment of process interaction, including but not limited to how it relates to opacity.

[40] Strictly local languages are essentially non-probabilistic n-gram models, and like n-grams, a string's k-factors overlap. For example, the 2-factors of CVC are #C, CV, VC, and C#.

As an example, consider a language that only allows syllables of the form CV, meaning all words in this language are of the form CV^n for some integer n. Abstracting away from individual consonant and vowel differences for simplicity, this language can be represented with the SL_2 grammar in (31):

(31) $\{\#V, CC, VV, C\#\}$

The reader can verify that all strings in CV^n are constructed from the 2-factors #C, CV, VC, and V#, none of which are in this grammar. Put another way, any string that violates this language's phonotactic constraints will contain at least one of the prohibited 2-factors in (31).

As proposed computational universals or at least strong tendencies, properties such as neighborhood-distinctness and strict locality serve to structure and restrict the hypothesis space a learner has to navigate, greatly reducing the number of generalizations it needs to consider. They have also served as the basis for provably correct learning algorithms that establish what kinds of patterns can be learned from data meeting certain criteria. Such proofs of correctness provide a guarantee that any pattern from any language that has the property in question can be learned, in contrast with simulation-based approaches in which success on particular languages and patterns must be assessed on a case-by-case basis.[41]

Heinz (2010b) expands on this approach in an FLT analysis of long-distance phonotactic dependencies – such as consonant harmony – that apply across an arbitrary number of intervening segments. While not SL, both symmetric and asymmetric long-distance agreement patterns can be described with strictly piecewise (SP) or precedence grammars, provided they do not involve blocking. A version of the string extension learner proposed in Heinz (2010a) for SL languages is shown to learn SP patterns in the limit from positive data. Furthermore, if long-distance agreement with blocking is unattested, as suggested by the typological surveys of Hansson (2001) and Rose and Walker (2004), the SP characterization provides an explanation for that gap.

An SP grammar differs from an SL grammar in that it contains the banned *subsequences*, or precedence relations among segments (i.e., segment x cannot precede segment y in a string, with potentially other segments intervening between them). Blocking patterns are out of reach because they place an added condition on whether a given subsequence is permitted: segment x cannot precede segment y *unless* segment z intervenes. Consider a sibilant harmony pattern in which [s] and [ʃ] cannot co-occur in a word unless [k] intervenes. The

---

[41] See Heinz (2011) for more discussion of algorithmic versus simulation-based approaches to phonological learning problems.

SP$_2$ grammar for such a language is shown in (32). (Remember the items in this grammar are interpreted as subsequences, not contiguous factors.)

(32)   {sʃ,ʃs}

If, however, the agreement is blocked by [k] – for example, if *sakaʃ* is well formed but *sapaʃ is not – then we have a contradiction. The subsequence *sʃ* must be in the grammar to rule out *sapaʃ, but that grammar will then also necessarily (and incorrectly) reject *sakaʃ*.[42] Thus the inability of SP to handle long-distance agreement with blocking combined with the typological prediction that such patterns are not possible suggests that precedence is a useful characterization of this category of phonotactic patterns.

However, subsequent work challenged that typological prediction with reported cases of long-distance agreement with blocking (e.g., Hansson 2010; Jurgec 2011). Based on such cases, McMullin (2016) argues that the tier-based strictly local (TSL) languages defined by Heinz et al. (2011) are a better characterization of long-distance patterns. Tier-based strictly local languages are defined with a subset of segments called the *tier*, over which SL constraints are defined. For example, sibilant harmony (without blocking) can be handled with a tier that includes only sibilants; the strings *sapaʃ* and *sapas* will be submitted to the grammar as just *sʃ* and *ss*, with non-tier segments removed. The SL$_2$ grammar in (33) then suffices to rule out the former and accept the latter.

(33)   {sʃ,ʃs}

Blocking is handled simply by including the blocking segments on the tier. In the example in which [k] blocks the sibilant harmony, the strings *sapaʃ and *sakaʃ* are correctly distinguished, because the former (*sʃ* with non-tier segments removed) but not the latter (*skʃ*) includes the banned sequence *sʃ*. As for learning, TSL can be learned by the same algorithms that learn SL, provided the tier is already known, but algorithms also exist for learning both the grammar and the tier (Jardine and Heinz 2016a; Jardine and McMullin 2017).

Heinz's (2010b) hypothesis that phonotactics are either SL or SP fit the assessment at the time that long-distance consonant agreement with blocking is unattested, and it also proposed an explanation for why that is the case (i.e., because of the way phonotactics are learned). The work on TSL that followed was motivated by a revision of that assessment, but equally important is what it revealed about

---

[42] One might think that raising the *k*-value to 3 will solve this problem, since we can then include *skʃ* in the grammar but omit *spʃ*. But the interleaving nature of subsequences means we can still construct an illegal word that satisfies this grammar: *sakasaʃakaʃ* includes the allowed sequence *skʃ* twice, with the [s] of the second token preceding the ʃ of the first one. The result is an *sʃ* subsequence without an intervening [k].

the formal relationship between competing models of phonotactic grammars.[43] Precedence versus tiers as defined by SP and TSL are not just notational variants or competing ways of thinking about locality; they are distinct, formally defined properties that either do or do not hold of a given pattern.[44] Neither property subsumes the other, as each can describe patterns the other cannot.[45]

An example of a pattern that is TSL but not SP was already discussed: consonant harmony with blocking. For an example that is SP but not TSL, consider a language with the alphabet {*a, b, c, d*} with two constraints: "a" cannot precede "b", and "b" cannot precede "c". This language is straightforwardly SP_2, as witnessed by the grammar in (34).

(34)   {*ab, bc*}

As a TSL_2 language, this pattern requires a tier of {*a, b, c*} and the same grammar interpreted as factors instead of subsequences. However, the string *acb*, in which an "a" precedes a "b", is incorrectly accepted, because its tier-string (also *acb*) contains neither of the banned factors.[46]

Formal language theory approaches to phonotactic learning traditionally forgo the use of statistics in favor of grammatical inference techniques that capitalize on the assumed structure of the hypothesis space. But Wilson and Gallagher (2018) argue that without statistics a feature-based model will be unable to determine which of the many possible feature representations are at the right level of specificity for the constraint it is trying to learn. For example, a language that enforces intervocalic voicing will allow sequences like [igi], [aba], and [ede], but will disallow *[iki], *[apa], and *[ete]. Some featural representations distinguish these two groups, such as $[-cons, +syl]$ $[+voice][-cons, +syl]$ versus $[-cons, +syl][-voice][-cons, +syl]$, but others do not, such as $[-cons, +syl][+cons][-cons, +syl]$, $[-cons, +syl][-son]$ $[-cons, +syl]$, or $[-cons, +syl][-cont][-cons, +syl]$, etcetera. Without

---

[43] The interest in TSL languages also inspired a series of extensions and applications to a variety of topics, including the coexistence of constraints on multiple tiers (Aksënova and Deshmukh 2018), morphotactic constraints (Aksënova et al. 2016), and even syntactic dependencies (Graf and Shafiei 2019; Vu et al. 2019).

[44] See also Lambert (2022, 2023) for an algebraic and model-theoretic approach to characterizing the type of relativized locality enacted by TSL.

[45] The search-copy model of vowel harmony (Mailhot and Reiss 2007; Nevins 2010) offers another comparison between precedence and locality in the context of processes. In this model, a recipient vowel searches for the first available donor vowel (i.e., its closest predecessor) that has the feature it needs to copy. By centralizing precedence, the model forgoes the need for any formal encoding of locality, including tiers. Furthermore, because underspecification is the impetus for a recipient vowel to initiate a search, blocking can still be handled with precedence by fully specifying opaque vowels.

[46] Thanks to Jeffrey Heinz (p.c.) for this example.

statistics to assess the accuracy of these competing constraints, the learner will not be able to converge on the correct one.

In response, Chandlee et al. (2019) and Rawski (2021) present a *structural inference* approach to this problem that exploits the inherent structure of the space of possible feature representations. In particular, substructures such as *k*-factors form a partial order: [+nasal] is a substructure of [+nasal, +voice], which is in turn a substructure of [+nasal, +voice, +labial], and so on. This inherent ordering among candidate constraints establishes the following grammatical entailments: if a structure is grammatical, so must be all of the structures it contains (i.e., sit below it in the order), and likewise if a structure is ungrammatical, so must be all of the structures that contain it (i.e., sit above it in the order).

The proposed algorithm (the bottom-up factor inference algorithm, or BUFIA) takes advantage of these entailments to greatly reduce the number of constraints it has to consider. As the name indicates, it proceeds bottom up through the order to first consider the "smallest" or most general constraints. If a structure is observed in the input data, then there cannot be a constraint against it, and so the algorithm moves on to the next structures in the order (e.g., if any [+nasal] segment exists, then *[+nasal] is rejected but $*[+nasal, +voice]$, $*[+nasal, -cont]$, etc. are still in the mix). In contrast, if no [+nasal] segment is found, then *[+nasal] can be kept as a constraint, and importantly, no constraint with [+nasal] as a substructure needs to be considered.

To address the redundancy in the set of constraints identified by this process (i.e., all constraints that are maximally general and equally describe the data will be returned), Rawski (2021) proposes additional abductive principles to prune the search space of constraints, including a requirement that an added constraint must rule out at least one new structure, or the stronger requirement that it must rule out an entirely new set of structures. Such principles share the goals of selection criteria like Hayes and Wilson's (2008) accuracy and generality or Wilson and Gallagher's (2018) measure of gain, but being situated in a deterministic learner they always find the same set of constraints.

7.2 Learning Input–Output Maps

In addition to the research on phonotactics, a parallel line of work in FLT has focused on the characterization and learning of input–output maps. As noted previously (Section 3.2.2), maps are *extensional* representations of phonological processes, whose properties hold regardless of the grammatical formalism that is chosen to encode them *intensionally*. This distinction between intensions and extensions is central to the phonological research grounded in

FLT. The finding that phonological grammars are regular was first based on an assumption that those grammars consist of a set of rules. Its further exploration in the context of constraint-based grammars (Section 3.3.1) was predicated on the idea that regularity should be preserved even without rules. Likewise, Tesar's (2014) ODL learner (Section 3.2.2) capitalized on a property of maps: OT grammars are not necessarily output driven, but those that are (i.e., those that generate an output-driven map) have learnability advantages. This section presents work that has similarly capitalized on the learnability advantages of subregular properties of maps.

The learning of maps, then, is distinct from the learning of rules: no particular rule formalism is assumed nor does it play any role in the learning algorithm. While test cases often refer to individual generalizations (e.g., final devoicing, intervocalic voicing, nasal assimilation, etc.) that one might represent inten-sionally with a rule, the target of the learner is still a map that could be generated by any number of grammatical devices. Furthermore, a single map can reflect the generalizations of multiple rules, even interacting ones (see Chandlee et al. 2018; Chandlee 2022). The learners surveyed in what follows in fact target *classes* of maps and will succeed on any map in its class, regardless of how many rules it represents.

The learnability advantage of subregularity for learning maps echoes the previous discussion of learning phonotactics: like the regular languages, the class of regular relations is insufficiently structured to guarantee learning from positive data. Functional counterparts to subregular languages have therefore been employed to address this problem. For example, the SL languages correspond to local functions (Berstel 1982; Vaysse 1986; Lind and Marcus 1995; see also Sakarovitch 2009), which compute the output string for a given input string based only on an examination of contiguous substrings (k-factors again) of bounded length. These functions are thus Markovian in that they can only make use of the most recent substring when deciding what to output next (with the degree of recentness determined by the size of k). The local functions have been further distinguished into two classes that differ in whether the examined substring is in the input or output string (Chandlee 2014), namely the input strictly local (ISL) and output strictly local (OSL) functions.[47] And just as the TSL languages augment the SL languages with the concept of a tier, tier-based counterparts to ISL and OSL have also been defined to model long-distance processes (Hao and Bowers 2019; Burness et al. 2021; Burness 2022).

---

[47] The difference in empirical coverage between input- and output-based locality can roughly be understood in terms of whether the "process iterates."

Algorithms exist for all of these classes that can identify any function in the target *k*-local class (Chandlee et al. 2014; Chandlee et al. 2015; Burness and McMullin 2019), or even any class that can be represented with a deterministic transducer (Jardine et al. 2014). Recent work has also tackled the problem of learning both the phonological map and the lexicon by decomposing the function that maps meanings to SRs into a meaning → UR lexicon function and the UR → SR phonological function (Hua et al. 2021; Hua and Jardine 2021). Again the learner capitalizes on the assumption that the phonological function is subregular – specifically *k*-ISL – to converge on its target grammar.

The algorithms proposed to establish the formal learnability of these classes serve to demonstrate how subregular properties structure the hypothesis space of functions in a way that enables learning from positive data. The proofs of learnability often take the form of first defining a characteristic or sufficient sample and then showing how the algorithm, when given data with that sample as a subset, is guaranteed to converge on the target function. But the often unrealistic nature of characteristic samples – including impossible sequences as well as not allowing for various sources of noise such as optionality, variation, and exceptions – means these algorithms are only the first step toward developing a viable phonological learning model.

For example, in Gildea and Jurafsky's (1996) experiments with a learning algorithm for subsequential functions (the onward subsequential transducer inference algorithm, or OSTIA; Oncina et al. 1993), they found that it cannot learn the English flapping rule even when given nearly 100,000 (input, output) string pairs derived from the CMU Pronunciation Dictionary. The issue is not the amount of data – OSTIA in fact requires little data compared to statistical learning models – but the type of data. Specifically, it would need to see whether flapping applies to impossible strings, such as /tɪt/. Gildea and Jurafsky's solution is to augment the learner with three phonologically informed learning biases: faithfulness (underlying segments undergo minimal changes), community (segments in natural classes tend to pattern together), and the use of context to identify phonological changes.

More recent work has explored additional routes for overcoming data limitations, including the use of semi-determinism (Beros and de la Higuera 2016) for optionality (Heinz 2020), as well as methods for generalizing over features (Markowska and Heinz 2023) and for identifying categorical constraints in the presence of exceptions (Dai 2022; Wu and Heinz 2023).

7.3 Model Theoretic Phonology

Much of the work mentioned so far has been grounded in the finite-state formalism, but other developments have demonstrated the utility of model theoretic approaches. Graf (2009, 2010) argues that the use of model theory for theory comparison is more efficient than an empirical approach, because theories (and variants of theories) can be grouped together based on how powerful a logic is needed to implement their assumptions. From there, we can assess what classes of phenomena a particular implementation accommodates, rather than separately testing individual patterns in individual theories. This type of investigation also provides a criterion for identifying the crucial distinctions among theories (which can be obscured given their extensive surface differences): specifically, the ones that necessitate an increase in logical power.

In addition, because logical characterizations operate over graphs, and strings are just a particular type of graph, model theory offers a straightforward way to extend string-based definitions of properties like locality to other structures, including nonlinear representations like trees, metrical grids (Liberman 1975; Liberman and Prince 1977; Prince 1983; Halle and Vergnaud 1987; Idsardi 1988; Hayes 1995), feature geometry (Sagey, 1986; Clements and Hume, 1995), and even sign (Rawski 2017).[48] For example, Jardine (2016b) presents a formal and restrictive theory of tone pattern well-formedness by applying a logical characterization of SL (i.e., the conjunction of negative literals, or CNL; see Strother-Garcia et al. 2016) to autosegmental graphs. Importantly, the use of logic allows the definition of locality to remain fixed while the representation is changed, highlighting the ways in which representation can modulate both perceived and formal pattern complexity.

As for input–output maps, logical characterizations of subregular function classes have been explored in work inspired by Engelfriet and Hoogeboom's (2001) finding that regular functions are equivalent to monadic second-order (MSO) graph interpretations (Enderton 1972).[49] The restrictions that define the different subregular function classes correspond to restrictions on the logic used for the interpretation. For example, Chandlee and Lindell (2016) show that as graph interpretations the ISL functions require only quantifier-free (QF) first-order (FO) logic. Chandlee and Jardine (2019, 2021) use this characterization of locality to define autosegmental input strictly local (AISL) functions for tone processes. An AISL function is a QF graph transduction over autosegmental graphs. They show how AISL enables a formal and nuanced investigation into the conditions under which ARs make a local

---

[48] In contrast, finite-state characterizations require distinct formal machinery when the representations go beyond simple strings – for example, Kornai's (1991) use of multi-tape transducers for autosegmental phonology (Goldsmith 1976).

[49] As noted previously (fn. 21), the use of the term *regular functions* here refers to the class of mappings generated by two-way deterministic FSTs, which are more expressive than the one-way FSTs used by Kaplan and Kay (1994).

analysis of long-distance tone processes possible, as some but not all are local over both strings and ARs, while others are local over only strings or only ARs.[50] Again, what it means to be local here is not impressionistic, but an exact criterion (namely, QF FO).

In addition, graph interpretation has also been a tool for assessing the significance of differences among alternative representations. For example, Strother-Garcia (2019) shows that three different syllable representations (i.e., trees, strings labeled with syllable positions, and strings with syllable boundaries marked) are all QF-bi-interpretable, meaning each can be converted into the other with a QF interpretation. Here the use of QF reflects the degree to which the differences between representations are meaningful. The fact that such a limited logic is sufficient for these conversions is taken as evidence that they are essentially notational equivalents. In the same vein, Oakden (2020) shows that Yip's (1989) and Bao's (1990) proposed tonal representations are also QF-bi-interpretable, Jardine et al. (2021) show that there is a FO-definable interpretation between constraints stated in Q-theory (Shih and Inkelas 2019) and those stated over ARs, and S. Nelson (2022) uses CNL and CPL (conjunction of positive literals) logics to establish the extensional equivalence of various feature systems.

Importantly, while the different characterizations of subregular languages and functions (i.e., finite-state versus logic; see also Lambert 2022 for an algebraic treatment) are based in distinct formalisms that have distinct advantages, they converge to define the exact same classes of objects.[51] Thinking about these objects in terms of these differing formalisms can only serve to deepen our understanding of the nature of the phonological patterns they represent. As Engelfriet and Hoogeboom (2001: 216) write, "It is always a pleasant surprise when two formalisms, introduced with different motivations, turn out to be equally powerful, as this indicates that the underlying concept is a natural one."

As noted by Heinz (2018), FLT offers a way to study phonology while being as atheoretical as one can get. This means we can gather insights into what phonology is – including predictions for what it can and cannot do, comparisons among different categories of patterns, and formally grounded criteria for what the relevant categories actually are – without being constrained by the lens of any one theory or formalism. This in turn allows us to uncover the aspects of our

---

[50] The AISL functions omit quantifiers and are also limited to referencing substructures in the input graph only. Relaxing that second restriction to allow reference to the output structure allows for a limited type of recursion that Chandlee and Jardine (2021) use as a logical approximation of the OSL functions.

[51] The finite-state characterizations have a decided advantage when it comes to establishing the learnability properties of these classes, as much more grammatical inference work has made use of finite-state representations compared to logic. See, for example, Heinz et al. (2015).

theories that do and do not reflect those independently discovered properties of our shared object of study. The finite-state treatments of SPE and OT mentioned previously are an example of this type of reckoning. More recently, work by Lamont (2019, 2021, 2022) has explored how the ways in which constraint-based grammars over-generate depend on different types of markedness constraints (local/substrings versus global/subsequences) and different versions of optimization (OT versus HS).

8 Conclusion

The variety and volume of work covered in this Element are a testament to how prevalent quantitative and computational approaches to phonology have become, and that trend is likely to not only continue but grow in the years ahead. Researchers focusing on a wide range of puzzles and problems related to the acquisition and representation of phonological knowledge are more fully embracing the value if not the necessity of computational, mathematical, and/or statistical tools in their investigations. In turn, these methods are becoming an increasingly necessary component of the teaching of and training in phonology as a field of study. The kinds of analysis they enable have greatly augmented our capacity for identifying and characterizing phonological patterns and for studying what can be learned under what conditions, from both a formal and an empirical perspective. Lastly, these approaches have equipped phonologists with a range of options for implementing our theories, forcing us to make them more precise and enabling us to better assess what remains to be uncovered with respect to the phonological component of natural languages.

References

Aksënova, A. (2020). Tool-Assisted Induction of Subregular Languages and Mappings. PhD thesis. Stony Brook University.

Aksënova, A. & Deshmukh, S. (2018). Formal restrictions on multiple tiers. In G. Jarosz, B. O'Connor & J. Pater, eds., *Proceedings of the Society for Computation in Linguistics*, Vol. 1, Article 8, pp. 64–73. https://aclanthology.org/W18-0307.

Aksënova, A., Graf, T. & Moradi, S. (2016). Morphotactics as tier-based strictly local dependencies. In M. Elsner & S. Kuebler, eds., *Proceedings of the Fourteenth SIGMORPHON Workshop on Computational Research in Phonetics, Phonology, and Morphology*. Berlin: Association for Computational Linguistics, pp. 121–30. https://aclanthology.org/W16-2019.

Albright, A. (2009). Feature-based generalisation as a source of gradient acceptability. *Phonology*, 26(1), 9–41.

Albright, A. & Hayes, B. (2002). Modeling English past tense intuitions with minimal generalization. In M. Maxwell, ed., *Proceedings of the ACL-02 Workshop on Morphological and Phonological Learning*. New Brunswick, NJ: Association for Computational Linguistics, pp. 58–69. https://aclanthology.org/W02-0607.

Albright, A. & Hayes, B. (2003). Rules vs. analogy in English past tenses: A computational/experimental study. *Cognition*, 90(2), 119–61.

Albright, A. & Hayes, B. (2014). Learning and learnability in phonology. In J. A. Goldsmith, J. Riggle & A. C. L. Yu, eds., *The Handbook of Phonological Theory*, 2nd ed. Hoboken, NJ: Wiley-Blackwell, pp. 661–90.

Alderete, J. & Tupper, P. (2018). Connectionist approaches to generative phonology. In A. Bosch & S. J. Hannahs, eds., *The Routledge Handbook of Phonological Theory*. New York: Routledge, pp. 360–90.

Alishahi, A., Barking, M. & Chrupała, G. (2017). Encoding of phonology in a recurrent neural model of grounded speech. In R. Levy & L. Specia, eds., *Proceedings of the Twenty-First Conference on Computational Natural Language Learning*. Vancouver: Association for Computational Linguistics, pp. 368–78. https://aclanthology.org/K17-1037.

Anderson, S. R. (1974). *The Organization of Phonology*. New York: Academic Press.

Anttila, A. (1997a). Deriving variation from grammar: A study of Finnish genitives. In F. Hinskens, R. van Hout & L. Wetzels, eds., *Variation, Change, and Phonological Theory*. Amsterdam: John Benjamins, pp. 35–68.

Anttila, A. (1997b). Variation in Finnish Phonology and Morphology. PhD thesis. Stanford University.

Anttila, A. (2008). Gradient phonotactics and the complexity hypothesis. *Natural Language & Linguistic Theory*, 26(4), 695–729.

Apoussidou, D. (2007). The Learnability of Metrical Phonology. PhD thesis. University of Amsterdam.

Armstrong, S. L., Gleitman, L. R. & Gleitman, H. (1983). What some concepts might not be. *Cognition*, 13(3), 263–308.

Bailey, T. (1995). Nonmetrical Constraints on Stress. PhD thesis. University of Minnesota.

Bailey, T. & Hahn, U. (2001). Determinants of wordlikeness: Phonotactics or lexical neighborhoods? *Journal of Memory and Language*, 44(4), 568–91.

Baković, E. (2000). Harmony, Dominance and Control. PhD thesis. Rutgers University.

Baković, E. & Blumenfeld, L. (2019). Rule interaction conversion operations. *Loquens*, 6.2, e062.

Bale, A. & Reiss, C. (2018). *Phonology: A Formal Introduction*. Cambridge, MA: MIT Press.

Bao, Z. (1990). On the Nature of Tone. PhD thesis, Massachusetts Institute of Technology.

Beesley, K. R. & Karttunen, L. (2003). *Finite State Morphology*. Stanford, CA: CSLI Publications.

Beguš, G. (2020a). Modeling unsupervised phonetic and phonological learning in generative adversarial phonology. In A. Ettinger, G. Jarosz & M. Nelson, eds., *Proceedings of the Society for Computation in Linguistics*, Vol. 3, Article 15. https://scholarworks.umass.edu/scil/vol3/iss1/15.

Beguš, G. (2020b). Generative adversarial phonology: Modeling unsupervised phonetic and phonological learning with neural networks. *Frontiers in Artificial Intelligence*, Vol. 3, Article 44. https://doi.org/10.3389/frai.2020.00044.

Belth, C. (2023). Towards a learning-based account of underlying forms: A case study in Turkish. In T. Hunter & B. Prickett, eds., *Proceedings of the Society for Computation in Linguistics*, Vol. 6, Article 31. https://scholarworks.umass.edu/scil/vol6/iss1/31.

Bermúdez-Otero R. (1999). Constraint Interaction in Language Change: Quantity in English and Germanic. PhD thesis. University of Manchester.

Bermúdez-Otero, R. (2003). The acquisition of phonological opacity. In J. Spenader, A. Eriksson & O. Dahl, eds., *Proceedings of the Stockholm Workshop on Variation within Optimality Theory*. Stockholm: Department of Linguistics, Stockholm University Press, pp. 25–36.

Beros, A. A. & de la Higuera, C. (2016). A canonical semi-deterministic transducer. *Fundamenta Informaticae*, 146(4), 431–59.

Berstel, J. (1982). Fonctions rationnelles et addition. *Actes de l'Ecole de Printemps de Théorie des Langages*. Paris: Laboratoire d'Informatique de Paris, pp. 177–83.

Bird, S. (1995). *Computational Phonology: A Constraint-Based Approach*. Cambridge: Cambridge University Press.

Bird, S., Coleman, J. S., Pierrehumbert, J. B. & Scobbie, J. M. (1992). Declarative phonology. In A. Crochetière, J.-C. Boulanger & C. Ouellon, eds., *Proceedings of the Fifteenth International Conference of Linguists*. Quebec: Presses de l'Université Laval.

Bird, S. & Ellison, T. M. (1994). One-level phonology: Autosegmental representations and rules as finite automata. *Computational Linguistics*, 20(1), 55–90. https://aclanthology.org/J94-1003.

Blaho, S. (2008). The Syntax of Phonology: A Radically Substance-Free Approach. PhD thesis. University of Tromso.

Boersma, P. (1997). How we learn variation, optionality, and probability. *Proceedings of the Institute of Phonetic Sciences of the University of Amsterdam*, 21, 43–58.

Boersma, P. (2001). Phonology–semantics interaction in OT, and its acquisition. In R. Kirchner, W. Wikeley & J. Pater, eds., *Papers in Experimental and Theoretical Linguistics*, 6. Edmonton: University of Alberta Press, pp. 24–35.

Boersma, P., Benders, T. & Seinhorst, K. (2020). Neural network models for phonology and phonetics. *Journal of Language Modelling*, 8(1), 103–77.

Boersma, P. & Hayes, B. (2001). Empirical tests of the gradual learning algorithm. *Linguistic Inquiry*, 32(1), 45–86.

Boersma, P. & Pater, J. (2016). Convergence properties of a gradual learning algorithm for harmonic grammar. In J. J. McCarthy & J. Pater, eds., *Harmonic Grammar and Harmonic Serialism*. London: Equinox, pp. 389–434.

Breiss, C. (2020). Constraint cumulativity in phonotactics: Evidence from artificial grammar learning studies. *Phonology*, 37(4), 551–76.

Breiss, C. & Albright, A. (2022). Cumulative markedness effects and (non-) linearity in phonotactics. *Glossa: A Journal of General Linguistics*, 7(1). https://doi.org/10.16995/glossa.5713.

Broe, M. (1993). Specification Theory: The Treatment of Redundancy in Generative Phonology. PhD thesis. University of Edinburgh.

Burness, P. (2022). Non-local Phonological Processes as Multi-tiered Strictly Local Maps. PhD thesis. University of Ottawa.

Burness, P. & McMullin, K. (2019). Efficient learning of output tier-based strictly 2-local functions. In P. de Groote, F. Drewes & G. Penn, eds., *Proceedings of the Sixteenth Meeting on the Mathematics of Language.* Toronto: Association for Computational Linguistics, pp. 78–90. https:// aclanthology.org/W19-5707.

Burness, P., McMullin, K. & Chandlee, J. (2021). Long-distance phonological processes as tier-based strictly local functions. *Glossa: A Journal of General Linguistics*, 6(1), 99. https://doi.org/10.16995/glossa.5780.

Bybee, J. (2001). *Phonology and Language Use.* Cambridge: Cambridge University Press.

Bybee, J. (2007). *Frequency of Use and the Organization of Language.* New York: Oxford Academic.

Calamaro, S. & Jarosz, G. (2015). Learning general phonological rules from distributional information: A computational model. *Cognitive Science*, 39(3), 647–66. https://doi.org/10.1111/cogs.12167.

Carden, G. (1983). The non-finite = state-ness of the word formation component. *Linguistic Inquiry*, 14(3), 537–41.

Chandlee, J. (2014). Strictly Local Phonological Processes. PhD thesis. University of Delaware.

Chandlee, J. (2022). Modulating between input and output locality: A case study on phonological opacity. In Ö. Bakay, B. Pratley, E. Neu & P. Deal, eds., *Proceedings of the Fifty-Second Annual Meeting of the North East Linguistic Society*, Vol. 1. Amherst, MA: Graduate Linguistics Student Association, pp. 119–38.

Chandlee, J., Eyraud, R. & Heinz, J. (2014). Learning strictly local subsequential functions. *Transactions of the Association for Computational Linguistics*, 2, 491–503. https://aclanthology.org/Q14-1038.

Chandlee, J., Eyraud, R. & Heinz, J. (2015). Output strictly local functions. In M. Kuhlmann, M. Kanazawa & G. M. Kobele, eds., *Proceedings of the Fourteenth Meeting on the Mathematics of Language.* Chicago, IL: Association for Computational Linguistics, pp. 112–25. https://aclanthol ogy.org/W15-2310.

Chandlee, J., Eyraud, R., Heinz, J., Jardine, A. & Rawski, J. (2019). Learning with partially ordered representations. In P. de Groote, F. Drewes & G. Penn, eds., *Proceedings of the Sixteenth Meeting on the Mathematics of Language.* Toronto: Association for Computational Linguistics, pp. 91–101. https:// aclanthology.org/W19-5708.

Chandlee, J., Heinz, J. & Jardine, A. (2018). Input strictly local opaque maps. *Phonology*, 35(2), 171–205.

Chandlee, J. & Jardine, A. (2019). Autosegmental input strictly local functions. *Transactions of the Association for Computational Linguistics*, 7, 157–68. https://aclanthology.org/Q19-1010.

Chandlee, J. & Jardine, A. (2021). Input and output locality and representation. *Glossa: A Journal of General Linguistics*, 6(1), 43. https://doi.org/10.5334/gjgl.1423.

Chandlee, J. & Jardine, A. (2022). Phonological theory and computational modelling. In B. E. Dresher & H. van der Hulst, eds., *The Oxford History of Phonology*. Oxford: Oxford University Press, pp. 656–76.

Chandlee, J. & Lindell, S. (2016). A logical characterization of strictly local functions. Paper presented at the Fourth Workshop on Natural Language and Computer Science. New York, July 10.

Chomsky, N. (1959). On certain formal properties of grammars. *Information and Control*, 2(2), 137–67.

Chomsky, N. & Halle, M. (1965). Some controversial questions in phonological theory. *Journal of Linguistics*, 1, 97–138.

Chomsky, N. & Halle, M. (1968). *Sound Pattern of English*. Cambridge, MA: MIT Press.

Chomsky, N. & Schützenberger, M. P. (1959). The algebraic theory of context-free languages. *Studies in Logic and the Foundations of Mathematics*, Vol. 26. Amsterdam: Elsevier, pp. 118–61.

Clements, G. N. & Hume, E. V. (1995). The internal organization of speech sounds. In J. Goldsmith, ed., *The Handbook of Phonological Theory*. Oxford: Blackwell, pp. 245–306.

Coetzee, A. W. (2006). Variation as accessing "non-optimal" candidates. *Phonology*, 23(3), 337–85.

Coetzee, A. W. & Pater, J. (2008). Weighted constraints and gradient restrictions on place co-occurrence in Muna and Arabic. *Natural Language & Linguistic Theory*, 26(2), 289–337.

Coleman, J. S. (1996). The psychological reality of language-specific constraints. Paper presented at the Fourth Phonology Meeting. University of Manchester, Manchester, UK, May 16–18.

Coleman, J. (2014). Phonology as computation. In J. A. Goldsmith, J. Riggle & A. C. L. Yu, eds., *The Handbook of Phonological Theory*, 2nd ed. Hoboken, NJ: Wiley-Blackwell, pp. 596–630.

Coleman, J. & Pierrehumbert, J. (1997). Stochastic phonological grammars and acceptability. In J. Coleman, ed., *Computational Phonology: Proceedings of the Third Meeting of the ACL Special Interest Group in Computational Phonology*. Madrid: Association for Computational Linguistics, pp. 49–56. https://aclanthology.org/W97-1107.

Çöltekin, Ç. (2010). A freely available morphological analyzer for Turkish. In N. Calzolari, K. Choukri, B. Maegaard, J. Mariani, J. Odijk, S. Piperidis, M. Rosner & D. Tapias, eds., *Proceedings of the Seventh International Conference on Language Resources and Evaluation*. Valletta, Malta: European Language Resources Association, pp. 820–7.

Culy, C. (1985). The complexity of the vocabulary of Bambara. *Linguistics and Philosophy*, 8(3), 345–51.

Dai, H. (2022). Phonotactic learning in the presence of exceptions with a categorical approach. Paper presented at the Annual Meeting on Phonology. University of California, Los Angeles, October 21–23.

Daland, R., Hayes, B., White, J., Garellek, M., Davis, A. & Norrmann, I. (2011). Explaining sonority projection effects. *Phonology*, 28(2), 197–234.

de la Higuera, C. (2010). *Grammatical Inference: Learning Automata and Grammars*. Cambridge: Cambridge University Press.

de Lacy, P. (2011). Markedness and faithfulness constraints. In M. van Oostendorp, C. J. Ewen, E. Hume & K. Rice, eds., *The Blackwell Companion to Phonology*. Hoboken, NJ: Wiley-Blackwell, pp. 1491–1512.

Dell, F. (1981). On the learnability of optional phonological rules. *Linguistic Inquiry*, 12(1), 31–7.

Dillon, B., Dunbar, E. & Idsardi, W. (2013). A single-stage approach to learning phonological categories: Insights from Inuktitut. *Cognitive Science*, 37(2), 344–77. https://doi.org/10.1111/cogs.12008.

Doucette, A. (2017). Inherent biases of recurrent neural networks for phonological assimilation and dissimilation. In T. Gibson, T. Linzen, A. Sayeed, M. van Schijndel & W. Schuler, eds., *Proceedings of the Seventh Workshop on Cognitive Modeling and Computational Linguistics*. Valencia, Spain: Association for Computational Linguistics, pp. 35–40. https://aclanthology.org/W17-0705.

Dresher, B. E. (1999). Charting the learning path: Cues to parameter setting. *Linguistic Inquiry*, 30(1), 27–67.

Dresher B. E. & Kaye, J. D. (1990). A computational learning model for metrical phonology. *Cognition*, 34(2), 137–95.

Durvasula, K. & Liter, A. (2020). There is a simplicity bias when generalizing from ambiguous data. *Phonology*, 37(2), 177–213.

Edlefsen, M., Leeman, D., Myers, N., Smith, N., Visscher, M. & Wellcome, D. (2008). Deciding strictly local (SL) languages. In J. Breitenbucher, ed., *Proceedings of the Midstates Conference for Undergraduate Research in Computer Science and Mathematics*. Wooster, OH: College of Wooster, pp. 66–73.

Eisenstat, S. (2009). Learning Underlying Forms with MaxEnt. Master's thesis. Brown University.

Eisner, J. (1997). Efficient generation in primitive optimality theory. In P. R. Cohen & W. Wahlster, eds., *Proceedings of the Thirty-Fifth Annual Meeting of the Association for Computational Linguistics and Eighth Conference of the European Chapter of the Association for Computational Linguistics*. Madrid: Association for Computational Linguistics, pp. 313–20. https://aclanthology.org/P97-1040.

Eisner, J. (2000). Directional constraint evaluation in optimality theory. In M. Kay, ed., *Proceedings of the Eighteenth International Conference on Computational Linguistics*. Saarbrucken, Germany: Association for Computational Linguistics, pp. 257–63. https://aclanthology.org/C00-1038.

Ellison, T. M. (1991). The iterative learning of phonological constraints. *Computational Linguistics*, 20(3), 1–32.

Ellison, T. M. (1992). The Machine Learning of Phonological Structure. PhD thesis. University of Western Australia.

Ellison, T. M. (1994). Phonological derivation in optimality theory. In M. Nagao, ed., *Proceedings of the Fifteenth International Conference on Computational Linguistics*, Vol. 2. Kyoto: Association for Computational Linguistics, pp. 1007–13. https://aclanthology.org/C94-2163.

Elsner, M., Goldwater, S. & Eisenstein, J. (2012). Bootstrapping a unified model of lexical and phonetic acquisition. In H. Li, C.-Y. Lin, M. Osborne, G. G. Lee & J. C. Park, eds., *Proceedings of the Fiftieth Annual Meeting of the Association for Computational Linguistics*, Vol. 1. Jeju Island, Korea: Association for Computational Linguistics, pp. 184–93. https://aclanthology.org/P12-1020.

Elsner, M., Goldwater, S., Feldman, N. & Wood, F. (2013). A joint learning model of word segmentation, lexical acquisition, and phonetic variability. In D. Yarowsky, T. Baldwin, A. Korhonen, K. Livescu & S. Bethard, eds., *Proceedings of the 2013 Conference on Empirical Methods in Natural Language Processing*. Seattle, WA: Association for Computational Linguistics, pp. 42–54. https://aclanthology.org/D13-1005.

Enderton, H. (1972). *A Mathematical Introduction to Logic*. Cambridge, MA: Academic Press.

Engelfriet, J. & Hoogeboom, H. J. (2001). MSO definable string transductions and two-way finite-state transducers. *ACM Transactions on Computational Logic*, 2, 216–54.

Filiot, E. & Reynier, P.-A. (2016). Transducers, logic and algebra for functions of finite words. *ACM SIGLOG News*, 3(3), 4–19.

Frank, R. & Satta, G. (1998). Optimality theory and the generative capacity complexity of constraint violability. *Computational Linguistics*, 24(2), 277–99. https://aclanthology.org/J98-2006.

Frisch, S. A., Pierrehumbert, J. B. & Broe, M. B. (2004). Similarity avoidance and the OCP. *Natural Language & Linguistic Theory*, 22(1), 179–228.

Futrell, R., Albright, A., Graff, P. & O'Donnell, T. J. (2017). A generative model of phonotactics. *Transactions of the Association for Computational Linguistics*, 5, 73–86. https://aclanthology.org/Q17-1006.

Gainor, B., Lai, R. & Heinz, J. (2012). Computational characterizations of vowel harmony patterns and pathologies. In J. Choi, E. A. Hogue, J. Punske, D. Tat, J. Schertz & A. Trueman, eds., *Proceedings of the Twenty-Ninth West Coast Conference on Formal Linguistics*. Somerville, MA: Cascadilla, pp. 63–71.

Galil, Z. & Megiddo, N. (1977). Cyclic ordering is NP-complete. *Theoretical Computer Science*, 5(2), 179–82.

Gasser, M. & Lee, C. (1990). *Networks and Morphophonemic Rules Revisited*. Technical report 307. Bloomington: Computer Science Department, Indiana University.

Gerdemann, D. & Hulden, M. (2012). Practical finite state optimality theory. In I. Alegria & M. Hulden, eds., *Proceedings of the Tenth International Workshop on Finite State Methods and Natural Language Processing*. Donostia-San Sebastian, Spain: Association for Computational Linguistics, pp. 10–19. https://aclanthology.org/W12-6202.

Gildea, D. & Jurafsky, D. (1996). Learning bias and phonological rule induction. *Computational Linguistics*, 22(4), 497–530. https://aclanthology .org/J96-4003.

Goedemans, R. W. N., Heinz, J. & van der Hulst, H. (2015). StressTyp2. http:// st2.ullet.net.

Gold, E. M. (1967). Language identification in the limit. *Information and Control*, 10(5), 447–74.

Goldsmith, J. (1976). Autosegmental Phonology. PhD thesis. Massachusetts Institute of Technology.

Goldsmith, J. (1992a). Grammar within a neural network. In S. D. Lima, R. L. Corrigan & G. K. Iverson, eds., *The Reality of Linguistic Rules: Proceedings of the Twenty-First Annual University of Wisconsin–Milwaukee Linguistics Symposium*. Amsterdam: John Benjamins, pp. 95–113.

Goldsmith, J. (1992b). Local modeling in phonology. In S. Davis, ed., *Connectionism: Theory and Practice*. Oxford: Oxford University Press, pp. 229–46.

Goldsmith, J. (2001). Unsupervised learning of the morphology of a natural language. *Computational Linguistics*, 27(2), 153–98. https://aclanthology.org/J01-2001.

Goldsmith, J. (2006). An algorithm for the unsupervised learning of morphology. *Natural Language Engineering*, 12(4), 353–71.

Goldsmith, J. & Larson, G. (1993). Using networks in a harmonic phonology. In C. Canakis, G. Chan & J. Denton, eds., *Papers from the Twenty-Eighth Regional Meeting of the Chicago Linguistic Society*, Vol. 2. Chicago, IL: Chicago Linguistic Society, pp. 94–125.

Goldsmith, J. & Riggle, J. (2012). Information theoretic approaches to phonological structure: The case of Finnish vowel harmony. *Natural Language & Linguistic Theory*, 30(3), 859–96.

Goldsmith, J. & Xanthos, A. (2009). Learning phonological categories. *Language*, 85(1), 4–38.

Goldwater, S. & Johnson, M. (2003). Learning OT constraint rankings using a maximum entropy model. In J. Spenader, A. Eriksson & O. Dahl, eds., *Proceedings of the Stockholm Workshop on Variation within Optimality Theory*. Stockholm: Stockholm University, Department of Linguistics, pp. 111–20.

Gordon, M. (2002). A factorial typology of quantity-insensitive stress. *Natural Language & Linguistic Theory*, 20(3), 491–552.

Gorman, K. (2013). Generative Phonotactics. PhD thesis. University of Pennsylvania.

Gorman, K. & Sproat, R. (2021). *Finite-State Text Processing*. Kentfield, CA: Morgan & Claypool.

Gouskova, M. & Gallagher, G. (2020). Inducing nonlocal constraints from baseline phonotactics. *Natural Language & Linguistic Theory*, 38(1), 77–116.

Graf, T. (2009). Towards a factorization of string-based phonology. In T. Icard, ed., *Proceedings of the Fourteenth Student Session of the European Summer School for Logic, Language, and Information*. Stanford, CA: Association for Logic, Language and Information, pp. 72–84.

Graf, T. (2010). Comparing incomparable frameworks: A model theoretic approach to phonology. *Proceedings of the Thirty-Third Annual Penn Linguistics Colloquium*, Vol. 16, Article 10. https://repository.upenn.edu/handle/20.500.14332/44749.

Graf, T. & Shafiei, N. (2019). C-command dependencies as TSL string constraints. In G. Jarosz, M. Nelson, B. O'Connor & J. Pater, eds., *Proceedings of the Society for Computation in Linguistics*, Vol. 2, Article 22. https://scholarworks.umass.edu/scil/vol2/iss1/22.

Greenberg, J. H. (1950). The patterning of root morphemes in Semitic. *Word*, 6(2), 162–81. https://doi.org/10.1080/00437956.1950.11659378.

Greenberg, J. H. & Jenkins, J. J. (1964). Studies in the psychological correlates of the sound system of American English. *Word*, 20(2), 157–77. https://doi.org/10.1080/00437956.1964.11659816.

Hale, M. & Reiss, C. (1998). Formal and empirical arguments concerning phonological acquisition. *Linguistic Inquiry*, 29(4), 656–83.

Hale, M. & Reiss, C. (2000a). Substance abuse and dysfunctionalism: Current trends in phonology. *Linguistic Inquiry*, 31(1), 157–69.

Hale, M. & Reiss, C. (2000b). Phonology as cognition. In N. Burton-Roberts, P. Carr & G. Docherty, eds., *Phonological Knowledge: Conceptual and Empirical Issues*. Oxford: Oxford University Press, pp. 161–84.

Hale, M. & Reiss, C. (2008). *The Phonological Enterprise*. Oxford: Oxford University Press.

Halle, M. (1959). *The Sound Pattern of Russian: A Linguistic and Acoustical Investigation*. The Hague: Mouton.

Halle, M. & Vergnaud, J.-R. (1987). *An Essay on Stress*. Cambridge, MA: MIT Press.

Hammond, M. (2003). Phonotactics and probabilistic ranking. In A. Carnie, H. Harley & M. Willie, eds., *Formal Approaches to Function in Grammar*. Amsterdam: John Benjamins, pp. 319–32.

Hammond, M. (2004). Gradience, phonotactics, and the lexicon in English phonology. *International Journal of English Studies*, 4(2), 1–24.

Hansson, G. Ó. (2001). Theoretical and Typological Issues in Consonant Harmony. PhD thesis. University of California, Berkeley.

Hansson, G. Ó. (2010). Long-distance voicing assimilation in Berber: Spreading and/or agreement? In M. Heijl, ed., *Actes du Congrès de l'ACL 2010/2010 CLA Conference Proceedings*. Montreal: Canadian Linguistic Association. https://cla-acl.ca/pdfs/actes-2010/CLA2010_Hansson.pdf.

Hao, S. (2019). Finite-state optimality theory: Non-rationality of harmonic serialism. *Journal of Language Modelling*, 7(2), 49–99.

Hao, S. (2024). Universal generation for optimality theory is PSPACE-complete. *Computational Linguistics*, 50(1), 83–117.

Hao, S. & Bowers, D. (2019). Action-sensitive phonological dependencies. In G. Nicolai & R. Cotterell, eds., *Proceedings of the Sixteenth Workshop on Computational Research in Phonetics, Phonology and Morphology*. Florence, Italy: Association for Computational Linguistics, pp. 218–28. https://aclanthology.org/W19-4225.

Hay, J., Pierrehumbert, J. & Beckman, M. E. (2004). Speech perception, well-formedness and the statistics of the lexicon. In J. Local, R. Ogden &

R. A. M. Temple, eds., *Phonetic Interpretation: Papers in Laboratory Phonology VI*. Cambridge: Cambridge University Press, pp. 58–74.

Hayes, B. (1995). *Metrical Stress Theory: Principles and Case Studies*. Chicago, IL: University of Chicago Press.

Hayes, B. (2004). Phonological acquisition in optimality theory: The early stages. In R. Kager, J. Pater & W. Zonneveld, eds., *Fixing Priorities: Constraints in Phonological Acquisition*. Cambridge: Cambridge University Press, pp. 158–203.

Hayes, B. & Londe, Z. (2006). Stochastic phonological knowledge: The case of Hungarian vowel harmony. *Phonology*, 23(1), 59–104.

Hayes, B. & White, J. (2013). Phonological naturalness and phonotactic learning. *Linguistic Inquiry*, 44(1), 45–75.

Hayes, B. & Wilson, C. (2008). A maximum entropy model of phonotactics and phonotactic learning. *Linguistic Inquiry*, 39(3), 379–440.

Heinz, J. (2007). The Inductive Learning of Phonotactic Patterns. PhD thesis. University of California, Los Angeles.

Heinz, J. (2009). On the role of locality in learning stress patterns. *Phonology*, 26(2), 303–51.

Heinz, J. (2010a). String extension learning. In J. Hajič, S. Carberry, S. Clark & J. Nivre, eds., *Proceedings of the Forty-Eighth Annual Meeting of the Association for Computational Linguistics*. Uppsala, Sweden: Association for Computational Linguistics, pp. 897–906. https://aclanthology.org/P10-1092.

Heinz, J. (2010b). Learning long-distance phonotactics. *Linguistic Inquiry*, 41(4), 623–61.

Heinz, J. (2011a). Computational phonology part I: Foundations. *Language and Linguistics Compass*, 5(4), 140–52.

Heinz, J. (2011b). Computational phonology part II: Grammars, learning, and the future. *Language and Linguistics Compass*, 5(4), 153–68.

Heinz, J. (2018). The computational nature of phonological generalizations. In L. Hyman & F. Plank, eds., *Phonological Typology: Phonetics and Phonology*. Berlin: De Gruyter Mouton, pp. 126–95.

Heinz, J. (2020). Deterministic analyses of optional processes. Talk given at University of Leipzig, December 9.

Heinz, J., de la Higuera, C. & van Zaanen, M. (2015). *Grammatical Inference for Computational Linguistics*. Synthesis Lectures on Human Language Technologies. Kentfield, CA: Morgan & Claypool.

Heinz, J. & Idsardi, W. (2011). Sentence and word complexity. *Science*, 333(6040), 295–7.

Heinz, J. & Idsardi, W. (2013). What complexity differences reveal about domains in language. *Topics in Cognitive Science*, 5(1), 111–31. https://doi.org/10.1111/tops.12000.

Heinz, J., Kobele, G. M. & Riggle, J. (2009). Evaluating the complexity of optimality theory. *Linguistic Inquiry*, 40(2), 277–88.

Heinz, J. & Lai, R. (2013). Vowel harmony and subsequentiality. In A. Kornai & M. Kuhlmann, eds., *Proceedings of the Thirteenth Meeting on the Mathematics of Language*. Sofia, Bulgaria: Association for Computational Linguistics, pp. 52–63. https://aclanthology.org/W13-3006.

Heinz, J., Rawal, C. & Tanner, H. G. (2011). Tier-based strictly local constraints for phonology. In D. Lin, Y. Matsumoto & R. Mihalcea, eds., *Proceedings of the Forty-Ninth Annual Meeting of the Association for Computational Linguistics*. Portland, OR: Association for Computational Linguistics, pp. 58–64. https://aclanthology.org/P11-2011.

Heinz, J. & Rawski, J. (2022). History of phonology: Learnability. In E. Dresher & H. van der Hulst, eds., *The Oxford History of Phonology*. Oxford: Oxford University Press, pp. 677–93.

Heinz, J. & Riggle, J. (2011). Learnability. In M. van Oostendorp, C. Ewen, E. Hume & K. Rice, eds., *Blackwell Companion to Phonology*. Hoboken, NJ: Wiley-Blackwell, pp. 54–78.

Heinz, J. & Sempere, J., eds. (2016). *Topics in Grammatical Inference*. Berlin: Springer.

Howard, I. (1972). A Directional Theory of Rule Application in Phonology. PhD thesis. MIT.

Hsu, B. (2022). Gradient symbolic representations in harmonic grammar. *Language & Linguistics Compass*, 16(9), e12473.

Hua, W. & Jardine, A. (2021). Learning input strictly local functions from their composition. In J. Chandlee, R. Eyraud, J. Heinz, A. Jardine & M. van Zaanen, eds., *Proceedings of the Fifteenth International Conference on Grammatical Inference*. PMLR 153, pp. 47–65. https://proceedings.mlr.press/v153/hua21a.html.

Hua, W., Jardine, A. & Dai, H. (2021). Learning underlying representations and input-strictly-local functions. In D. K. E. Reisinger & M. Huijsmans, eds., *Proceedings of the Thirty-Seventh West Coast Conference on Formal Linguistics*. Somerville, MA: Cascadilla, pp. 143–51.

Hulden, M. (2009). Foma: A finite-state compiler and library. In J. Kreutel, ed., *Proceedings of the Demonstrations Session at EACL 2009*. Athens: Association for Computational Linguistics, pp. 29–32. https://aclanthology.org/E09-2008.

Idsardi, W. J. (1988). The Computation of Prosody. PhD thesis. Massachusetts Institute of Technology.

Idsardi, W. J. (2006). A simple proof that optimality theory is computationally intractable. *Linguistic Inquiry*, 37(2), 271–5.

Idsardi, W. J. (2009). Calculating metrical structure. In E. Raimy and C. E. Cairns, eds., *Contemporary Views on Architecture and Representations in Phonology*. Cambridge, MA: MIT Press, pp. 191–211.

Inkelas, S., Orgun, C. O. & Zoll, C. (1997). The implications of lexical exceptions for the nature of grammar. In I. Roca, ed., *Derivations and Constraints in Phonology*. Oxford: Clarendon, pp. 393–418.

Ito, J. & Mester, A. (2003). *Japanese Morphophonemics: Markedness and Word Structure*. Cambridge, MA: MIT Press.

Jäger, G. (2007). Maximum entropy models and stochastic optimality theory. In A. Zaenen, J. Simpson, T. Holloway King, J. Grimshaw, J. Maling & C. Manning, eds., *Architectures, Rules, and Preferences: A Festschrift for Joan Bresnan*. Stanford, CA: Center for the Study of Language and Information, pp. 467–79.

Jain, S., Osherson, D., Royer, J. S. & Sharma, A. (1999). *Systems That Learn: An Introduction to Learning Theory (Learning, Development and Conceptual Change)*, 2nd ed. Cambridge, MA: MIT Press.

Jardine, A. (2016a). Computationally, tone is different. *Phonology*, 33(2), 247–83.

Jardine, A. (2016b). Locality and Non-linear Representations in Tonal Phonology. PhD thesis. University of Delaware.

Jardine, A., Chandlee, J., Eyraud, R. & Heinz, J. (2014). Very efficient learning of structured classes of subsequential functions from positive data. In A. Clark, M. Kanazawa & R. Yoshinaka, eds., *Proceedings of the Twelfth International Conference on Grammatical Inference*. PMLR 34, pp. 94–108. https://proceedings.mlr.press/v34/jardine14a.html.

Jardine, A., Danis, N. & Iacoponi, L. (2021). A formal investigation of Q-theory in comparison to autosegmental representations. *Linguistic Inquiry*, 52(2), 333–58.

Jardine, A. & Heinz, J. (2016a). Learning tier-based strictly 2-local languages. *Transactions of the Association for Computational Linguistics*, 4, 87–98. https://aclanthology.org/Q16-1007.

Jardine, A. & Heinz, J. (2016b). Markedness constraints are negative: An autosegmental constraint definition language. In K. Ershova, J. Falk, J. Geiger, Z. Hebert, R. E. Lewis Jr., P. Munoz, J. B. Phillips & B. Pillion, eds., *Proceedings of the Fifty-First Annual Meeting of the Chicago Linguistic Society*. Chicago, IL: Chicago Linguistic Society, pp. 301–15.

Jardine, A. & McMullin, K. (2017). Efficient learning of tier-based strictly *k*-local languages. In F. Drewes, C. Martín-Vide & B. Truthe, eds., *Proceedings of Language and Automata Theory and Applications, 11th International Conference*. New York: Springer, pp. 64–76.

Jarosz, G. (2006a). Richness of the base and probabilistic unsupervised learning in optimality theory. In R. Wicentowski & G. Kondrak, eds., *Proceedings of the Eighth Meeting of the ACL Special Interest Group on Computational Phonology and Morphology*. New York: Association for Computational Linguistics, pp. 50–9. https://aclanthology.org/W06-3207.

Jarosz, G. (2006b). Rich Lexicons and Restrictive Grammars: Maximum Likelihood Learning in Optimality Theory. PhD thesis. Johns Hopkins University.

Jarosz, G. (2009). Restrictiveness and phonological grammar and lexicon learning. In M. Elliot, J. Kirby, O. Sawada, E. Staraki & S. Yoon, eds., *Proceedings of the Forty-Third Annual Meeting of the Chicago Linguistic Society*. Chicago, IL: Chicago Linguistic Society, pp. 123–37.

Jarosz, G. (2014). Serial markedness reduction. In J. Kingston, C. Moore-Cantwell, J. Pater & R. Staubs, eds., *Proceedings of the 2013 Annual Meeting on Phonology*. Washington, DC: Linguistic Society of America. https://doi.org/10.3765/amp.v1i1.40.

Jarosz, G. (2016). Learning opaque and transparent interactions in harmonic serialism. In G. Ó. Hansson, A. Farris-Trimble, K. McMullin & D. Pulleyblank, eds., *Proceedings of the 2015 Annual Meeting on Phonology*. Washington, DC: Linguistic Society of America. https://doi.org/10.3765/amp.v3i0.3671.

Jarosz, G. (2019). Computational modeling of phonological learning. In *Annual Review of Linguistics*, 5, 67–90. https://doi.org/10.1146/annurev-linguistics-011718-011832.

Jesney, K. & Tessier, A.-M. (2009). Gradual learning and faithfulness: Consequences of ranked vs. weighted constraints. In M. Abdurrahman, A. Schardl & M. Walkow, eds., *Proceedings of the Thirty-Eighth Meeting of the North East Linguistic Society*. Amherst, MA: Graduate Linguistics Student Association, pp. 449–62.

Johnson, C. D. (1972). *Formal Aspects of Phonological Description*. The Hague: Mouton.

Johnson, M. (1984). A discovery procedure for certain phonological rules. In Y. Wilks, ed., *Proceedings of the Tenth International Conference on Computational Linguistics and the Twenty-Second Annual Meeting of the Association for Computational Linguistics*. Stanford, CA: Association for Computational Linguistics, pp. 344–7. https://aclanthology.org/P84-1070.

Jurafsky, D. & Martin, J. (2008). *Speech and Language Processing*, 2nd ed. Hoboken, NJ: Prentice Hall.

Jurgec, P. (2011). Feature Spreading 2.0: A Unified Theory of Assimilation. PhD thesis. University of Tromso.

Kahng, J. & Durvasula, K. (2023). Can you judge what you don't hear? Perception as a source of gradient wordlikeness judgements. *Glossa: A Journal of General Linguistics*, 8(1). https://doi.org/10.16995/glossa.9333.

Kaplan, R. & Kay, M. (1994). Regular models of phonological rule systems. *Computational Linguistics*, 20(3), 331–78. https://aclanthology.org/J94-3001.

Karttunen, L. (1998). The proper treatment of optimality in computational phonology. In L. Karttunen & K. Oflazer, eds., *Proceedings of the International Workshop on Finite State Methods in Natural Language Processing*. Ankara, Turkey: Bilkent University, pp. 1–12. https://aclanthology.org/W98-1301.

Keane, J., Sehyr, Z., Emmorey, K. & Brentari, D. (2017). A theory-driven model of handshape similarity. *Phonology*, 34(2), 221–41.

Kenstowicz, M. & Kisseberth, C. (1977). *Topics in Phonological Theory*. New York: Academic Press.

Kenstowicz, M. & Kisseberth, C. (1979). *Generative Phonology: Description and Theory*. New York: Academic Press.

Kiparsky, P. (1968). Linguistic universals and linguistic change. In E. Bach & R. T. Harms, eds., *Universals in Linguistic Theory*. New York: Holt, Rinehart & Winston, pp. 170–202.

Kiparsky, P. (1971). Historical linguistics. In W. O. Dingwall, ed., *A Survey of Linguistic Science*. College Park: University of Maryland Linguistics Program, pp. 576–642.

Kiparsky, P. (2000). Opacity and cyclicity. *The Linguistic Review*, 17(2–4), 351–65.

Kobele, G. (2006). Generating Copies: An Investigation into Structural Identity in Language and Grammar. PhD thesis. University of California, Los Angeles.

Kornai, A. (1991). Formal Phonology. PhD thesis. Stanford University.

Kornai, A. (2009). The complexity of phonology. *Linguistic Inquiry*, 40(4), 701–12.

Koskenniemi, K. (1983). *Two-Level Morphology*. Publication no. 11, Department of General Linguistics. Helsinki: University of Helsinki.

Lambert, D. (2022). Unifying Classification Schemes for Languages and Processes with Attention to Locality and Relativizations Thereof. PhD thesis. Stony Brook University.

Lambert, D. (2023). Relativized adjacency. *Journal of Logic, Language and Information*, 32, 707–31.

Lamont, A. (2019). Precedence is pathological: The problem of alphabetical sorting. In R. Stockwell, M. O'Leary, Z. Xu & Z. L. Zhou, eds., *Proceedings of the Thirty-Sixth West Coast Conference on Formal Linguistics*. Somerville, MA: Cascadilla, pp. 243–9.

Lamont, A. (2021). Optimizing over subsequences generates context-sensitive languages. *Transactions of the Association for Computational Linguistics*, 9, 528–37. https://aclanthology.org/2021.tacl-1.32.

Lamont, A. (2022). Optimality theory implements complex functions with simple constraints. *Phonology*, 38(4), 729–74.

Leben, W. (1973). Suprasegmental Phonology. PhD thesis. Massachusetts Institute of Technology.

Legendre, G., Miyata, Y. & Smolensky, P. (1990). Can connectionism contribute to syntax? Harmonic grammar, with an application. In M. Ziolkowski, M. Noske & K. Deaton, eds., *Papers from the Twenty-Sixth Regional Meeting of the Chicago Linguistic Society*, Vol. 1. Chicago, IL: Chicago Linguistic Society, pp. 237–52.

Liberman, M. (1975). The Intonational System of English. PhD thesis. Massachusetts Institute of Technology.

Liberman, M. & Prince, A. (1977). On stress and linguistic rhythm. *Linguistic Inquiry*, 8(2), 249–336.

Lind, D. & Marcus, B. (1995). *Symbolic Dynamics and Coding*. Cambridge: Cambridge University Press.

Linzen, T. & O'Donnell, T. J. (2015). A model of rapid phonotactic generalization. In L. Màrquez, C. Callison-Burch & J. Su, eds., *Proceedings of the 2015 Conference on Empirical Methods in Natural Language Processing*. Lisbon: Association for Computational Linguistics, pp. 1126–31. https://aclanthology.org/D15-1134.

Lombardi, L. (1999). Positional faithfulness and voicing assimilation in optimality theory. *Natural Language & Linguistic Theory*, 17(2), 267–302.

Magri, G. (2012). Convergence of error-driven ranking algorithms. *Phonology*, 29(2), 213–69.

Magri, G. (2013a). The complexity of learning in OT and its implications for the acquisition of phonotactics. *Linguistic Inquiry*, 44(3), 433–68.

Magri, G. (2013b). HG has no computational advantages over OT: Toward a new toolkit for computational OT. *Linguistic Inquiry*, 44(4), 569–609.

Magri, G. (2016). Error-driven learning in optimality theory and harmonic grammar: A comparison. *Phonology*, 33(3), 493–532.

Mailhot, F. & Reiss, C. (2007). Computing long-distance dependencies in vowel harmony. *Biolinguistics*, 1. https://doi.org/10.5964/bioling.8587.

Markowska, M. & Heinz, J. (2023). Empirical and theoretical arguments for using properties of letters for the learning of sequential functions. In F. Coste, F. Ouardi & G. Rabusseau, eds., *Proceedings of the Sixteenth International Conference on Grammatical Inference*. PMLR 217, pp. 270–4. https://proceedings.mlr.press/v217/markowska23a/markowska23a.pdf.

Matusevych, Y., Schatz, T., Kamper, H., Feldman, N. H. & Goldwater, S. (2023). Infant phonetic learning as perceptual space learning: A crosslinguistic evaluation of computational models. *Cognitive Science*, 47(7), e13314. https://doi.org/10.1111/cogs.13314.

Mayer, C. (2020). An algorithm for learning phonological classes from distributional similarity. *Phonology*, 37(1), 91–131.

Mayer, C. & Daland, R. (2020). A method for projecting features from observed sets of phonological classes. *Linguistic Inquiry*, 51(4), 725–63.

Mayer, C. & Nelson, M. (2020). Phonotactic learning with neural language models. In A. Ettinger, G. Jarosz & M. Nelson, eds., *Proceedings of the Society for Computation in Linguistics*, Vol. 3, Article 16. https://scholarworks.umass.edu/scil/vol3/iss1/16.

McCarthy, J. J. (2000). Harmonic serialism and parallelism. In M. Hirotani, A. Coetzee, N. Hall & J. Kim, eds., *Proceedings of the Thirtieth Annual Meeting of the North East Linguistic Society*, Vol. 2. Amherst, MA: Graduate Linguistics Student Association, pp. 501–24. https://scholarworks.umass.edu/nels/vol30/iss2/8.

McCollum, A. G., Baković, E., Mai, A. & Meinhardt, E. (2020). Unbounded circumambient patterns in segmental phonology. *Phonology*, 37(2), 215–55.

McMullin, K. (2016). Tier-Based Locality in Long-Distance Phonotactics: Learnability and Typology. PhD thesis. University of British Columbia.

McNaughton, R. & Papert, S. (1971). *Counter-Free Automata*. Cambridge, MA: MIT Press.

Meinhardt, E., Mai, A., Baković, E. & McCollum, A. (2024). Weak determinism and the computational consequences of interaction. *Natural Language & Linguistic Theory*. https://doi.org/10.1007/s11049-023-09578-1.

Merchant, N. (2008). Discovering Underlying Forms: Contrast Pairs and Ranking. PhD thesis. Rutgers University.

Merchant, N. & Tesar, B. (2008). Learning underlying forms by searching restricted lexical subspaces. In R. L. Edwards, P. J. Midtlyng, C. L. Sprague & K. G. Stensrud, eds., *Proceedings of the Forty-First Meeting of the Chicago Linguistic Society*, Vol. 2. Chicago, IL: Chicago Linguistic Society, pp. 33–47.

Merrill, W. (2023). Formal languages and the NLP black box. In F. Drewes & M. Volkov, eds., *Developments in Language Theory*. New York: Springer, pp. 1–8.

Mielke, J. (2008). *The Emergence of Distinctive Features*. Oxford: Oxford University Press.

Mohri, M. (1997). Finite-state transducers in language and speech processing. *Computational Linguistics*, 23(2), 269–311. https://aclanthology.org/J97-2003.

Mohri, M., Rostamizadeh, A. & Talwalkar, A. (2018). *Foundations of Machine Learning*, 2nd ed. Cambridge, MA: MIT Press.

Moore-Cantwell, C. & Pater, J. (2016). Gradient exceptionality in maximum entropy grammar with lexically specific constraints. *Catalan Journal of Linguistics*, 15, 53–66. https://doi.org/10.5565/rev/catjl.183.

Nazarov, A. (2016). Extending Hidden Structure Learning: Features, Opacity, and Exceptions. PhD thesis. University of Massachusetts, Amherst.

Nazarov, A. & Pater, J. (2017). Learning opacity in stratal maximum entropy grammar. *Phonology*, 34(2), 299–324.

Nelson, M. (2019). Segmentation and UR acquisition with UR constraints. In G. Jarosz, M. Nelson, B. O'Connor & J. Pater, eds., *Proceedings of the Society for Computation in Linguistics*, Vol. 2, Article 8. https://scholar works.umass.edu/scil/vol2/iss1/8.

Nelson, M. (2022). Phonotactic Learning with Distributional Representations. PhD thesis. University of Massachusetts, Amherst.

Nelson, S. (2022). A model theoretic perspective on phonological feature systems. In A. Ettinger, T. Hunter & B. Prickett, eds., *Proceedings of the Society for Computation in Linguistics*, Vol. 5, Article 2. https://scholar works.umass.edu/scil/vol5/iss1/2.

Nevins, A. (2010). *Locality in Vowel Harmony*. Cambridge, MA: MIT Press.

Nyman, A. & Tesar, B. (2019). Determining underlying presence in the learning of grammars that allow insertion and deletion. *Glossa: A Journal of General Linguistics*, 4(1), 37. https://doi.org/10.5334/gjgl.603.

Oakden, C. (2020). Notational equivalence in tonal geometry. *Phonology*, 37(2), 257–96.

Odden, D. (2022). Radical substance-free phonology and feature learning. *The Canadian Journal of Linguistics/La revue canadienne de linguistique*, 67(4), pp. 500–51.

Ohala, J. J. & Ohala, M. (1986). Testing hypotheses regarding the psychological manifestation of morpheme structure constraints. In J. J. Ohala & J. J. Jaeger, eds., *Experimental Phonology*. Cambridge, MA: Academic Press, pp. 239–52.

O'Hara, C. (2017). How abstract is more abstract? Learning abstract underlying representations. *Phonology*, 34(2), 325–45.

Oncina, J., García, P. & Vidal, E. (1993). Learning subsequential transducers for pattern recognition tasks. *IEEE Transactions on Pattern Analysis and Machine Intelligence*, 15(5), 448–58.

Osherson, D., Weinstein, S. & Stob, M. (1986). *Systems That Learn*. Cambridge, MA: MIT Press.

Padgett, J. (1995). Partial class behavior and nasal place assimilation. In K. Suzuki & D. Elzinga, eds., *Proceedings of the South Western Optimality Theory Workshop*. http://hdl.handle.net/10150/227277.

Pater, J. (2008). Gradual learning and convergence. *Linguistic Inquiry*, 39(2), 334–45.

Pater, J. (2009). Weighted constraints in generative linguistics. *Cognitive Science*, 33(6), 999–1035. https://doi.org/10.1111/j.1551-6709.2009.01047.x.

Pater, J. (2019). Generative linguistics and neural networks at 60: Foundation, friction, and fusion. *Language*, 95(1), e41–74.

Pater, J., Jesney, K., Staubs, R. D. & Smith, B. (2012). Learning probabilities over underlying representations. In L. Cahill & A. Albright, eds., *Proceedings of the Twelfth Meeting of the Special Interest Group on Computational Morphology and Phonology*. Montreal: Association for Computational Linguistics, pp. 62–71. https://aclanthology.org/W12-2308.

Peperkamp, S., Le Calvez, R., Nadal, J.-P. & Dupoux, E. (2006). The acquisition of allophonic rules: Statistical learning with linguistic constraints. *Cognition*, 101(3), B31–41.

Pierrehumbert, J. (2001a). Exemplar dynamics: Word frequency, lenition and contrast. In J. Bybee & P. Hopper, eds., *Frequency and the Emergence of Linguistic Structure*. Amsterdam: John Benjamins, pp. 137–57.

Pierrehumbert, J. (2001b). Stochastic phonology. *GLOT*, 5(6), 1–13.

Pinker, S. & Prince, A. (1994). Regular and irregular morphology and the psychological status of rules of grammar. In S. D. Lima, R. L. Corrigan & G. K. Iverson, eds., *The Reality of Linguistic Rules*. Amsterdam: John Benjamins, pp. 321–52.

Potts, C. & Pullum, G. K. (2002). Model theory and the content of OT constraints. *Phonology*, 19(3), 361–93.

Prickett, B. (2019). Learning biases in opaque interactions. *Phonology*, 36(4), 627–53.

Prickett, B. (2021). Modelling a subregular bias in phonological learning with recurrent neural networks. *Journal of Language Modelling*, 9(1), 67–96. https://doi.org/10.15398/jlm.v9i1.251.

Prickett, B. & Pater, J. (2022). Learning stress patterns with a sequence-to-sequence neural network. In A. Ettinger, T. Hunter & B. Prickett, eds.,

Proceedings of the Society for Computation in Linguistics, Vol. 5, Article 10. https://aclanthology.org/2022.scil-1.9.

Prince, A. (1983). Relating to the grid. *Linguistic Inquiry*, 14(1), 19–100.

Prince, A. (2000). Comparative Tableaux. Master's thesis. Rutgers University. ROA-376.

Prince, A. & Smolensky, P. (1993). *Optimality Theory: Constraint Interaction in Generative Grammar*. Technical Report 2. New Brunswick, NJ: Rutgers University Center for Cognitive Science.

Prince, A. & Smolensky, P. (2004). *Optimality Theory: Constraint Interaction in Generative Grammar*. Hoboken, NJ: Wiley-Blackwell.

Prince, A. & Tesar, B. (2004). Learning phonotactic distributions. In R. Kager, J. Pater & W. Zonneveld, eds., *Constraints in Phonological Acquisition*. Cambridge: Cambridge University Press, pp. 245–91.

Rasin, E., Berger, I., Lan, N., Shefi, I. & Katzir, R. (2021). Approaching explanatory adequacy in phonology using minimum description length. *Journal of Language Modelling*, 9(1), 17–66. https://doi.org/10.15398/jlm .v9i1.266.

Rasin, E. & Katzir, R. (2016). On evaluation metrics in optimality theory. *Linguistic Inquiry*, 47(2), 235–82.

Rasin, E., Shefi, I. & Katzir, R. (2020). A unified approach to several learning challenges in phonology. In M. Asatryan, Y. Song & A. Whitmal, eds., *Proceedings of the Fiftieth Meeting of the North East Linguistic Society*, Vol. 3. Amherst, MA: Graduate Linguistics Student Association, pp. 73–87.

Rawski, J. (2017). Phonological complexity across speech and sign. In D. Edmiston, M. Ermolaeva, E. Hakgüder, J. Lai, K. Montemurro, B. Rhodes, A. Sankhagowit & M. Tabatowski, eds., *Proceedings of the Fifty-Third Annual Meeting of the Chicago Linguistic Society*. Chicago, IL: Chicago Linguistic Society, pp. 307–20.

Rawski, J. (2021). Structure and Learning in Natural Language. PhD thesis. Stony Brook University.

Reiss, C. (2008). Constraining the learning path without constraints, or The Ocp and NoBanana. In B. Vaux & A. Nevins, eds., *Rules, Constraints, and Phonological Phenomena*. Oxford: Oxford University Press, pp. 252–302.

Riggle, J. (2004). Generation, Recognition, and Learning in Finite State Optimality Theory. PhD thesis. University of California, Los Angeles.

Riggle, J. & Wilson, C. (2006). Local optionality. In L. Bateman & C. Ussery, eds., *Proceedings of the Thirty-Fifth Annual Meeting of the North East Linguistic Society*, Vol. 2. Amherst, MA: Graduate Linguistics Student Association, pp. 539–50.

Rogers, J., Heinz, J., Bailey, G., Edlefsen, M., Visscher, M., Wellcome, D. & Wibel, S. (2010). On languages piecewise testable in the strict sense. In C. Ebert, G. Jäger & J. Michaelis, eds., *The Mathematics of Language*. New York: Springer, pp. 255–65.

Rogers, J. & Lambert, D. (2019). Extracting subregular constraints from regular stringsets. *Journal of Language Modelling*, 7(2), 143–76.

Rogers, J. & Pullum, G. (2011). Aural pattern recognition experiments and the subregular hierarchy. *Journal of Logic, Language and Information*, 20, 329–42.

Rose, S. & Walker, R. (2004). A typology of consonant agreement as correspondence. *Language*, 80(3), 475–531.

Rumelhart, D. E. & McClelland, J. L. (1986). On learning the past tenses of English verbs. In D. E. Rumelhart & J. L. McClelland, eds., *Parallel Distributed Processing: Explorations in the Microstructures of Cognition*, Vol. 2. Cambridge, MA: MIT Press, pp. 216–71.

Sagey, E. (1986). The Representation of Features and Relations in Non-linear Phonology. PhD thesis. Massachusetts Institute of Technology.

Sakarovitch, J. (2009). *Elements of Automata Theory*. Cambridge: Cambridge University Press.

Schwarz, G. (1978). Estimating the dimension of a model. *The Annals of Statistics*, 6(2), 461–4.

Scobbie, J. M., Coleman, J. S. & Bird, S. (1996). Key aspects of declarative phonology. In J. Durand & B. Laks, eds., *Current Trends in Phonology: Models and Methods*, Vol. 2. Manchester, UK: ESRI, University of Salford, pp. 685–709.

Shademan, S. (2006). Is phonotactic knowledge grammatical knowledge? In D. Baumer, D. Montero and M. Scanlon, eds., *Proceedings of the Twenty-Fifth West Coast Conference on Formal Linguistics*. Somerville, MA: Cascadilla, pp. 371–9.

Shieber, S. (1985). Evidence against the context-freeness of natural language. *Linguistics and Philosophy*, 8, 333–43.

Shih, S. (2017). Constraint conjunction in weighted probabilistic grammar. *Phonology*, 34(2), 243–68.

Shih, S. & Inkelas, S. (2016). Morphologically-conditioned tonotactics in multilevel maximum entropy grammar. In G. Ó. Hansson, A. Farris-Trimble, K. McMullin & D. Pulleyblank, eds., *Proceedings of the 2015 Annual Meeting on Phonology*. Washington, DC: Linguistic Society of America. https://doi.org/10.3765/amp.v3i0.3659.

Shih, S. & Inkelas, S. (2019). Autosegmental aims in surface-optimizing phonology. *Linguistic Inquiry*, 50(1), 137–96.

Smith, B. & Pater, J. (2020). French schwa and gradient cumulativity. *Glossa: A Journal of General Linguistics*, 5(1), 24. https://doi.org/10.5334/gjgl.583.

Smith, C. (2018). Harmony in Gestural Phonology. PhD thesis. University of Southern California.

Smith, C., O'Hara, C., Rosen, E. & Smolensky, P. (2021). Emergent gestural scores in a recurrent neural network model of vowel harmony. In A. Ettinger, E. Pavlich & B. Prickett, eds., *Proceedings of the Society for Computation in Linguistics*, Vol. 4, Article 7. https://scholarworks.umass.edu/scil/vol4/iss1/7.

Smolensky, P. (1996). On the comprehension/production dilemma in child language. *Linguistic Inquiry*, 27(4), 720–31.

Smolensky, P. & Goldrick, M. (2016). Gradient Symbolic Representations in Grammar: The Case of French Liaison. Master's thesis. Johns Hopkins University of Northwestern University. ROA-1286. https://roa.rutgers.edu/content/article/files/1552_smolensky_1.pdf.

Smolensky, P., Goldrick, M. & Mathis, D. (2014). Optimization and quantization in gradient symbol systems: A framework for integrating the continuous and the discrete in cognition. *Cognitive Science*, 38(6), 1102–38. https://doi.org/10.1111/cogs.12047.

Smolensky, P. & Legendre, G. (2006). *The Harmonic Mind: From Neural Computation to Optimality-Theoretic Grammar*. Cambridge, MA: MIT Press.

Stanley, R. (1967). Redundancy rules in phonology. *Language*, 43(2), 393–436.

Staubs, R. D. & Pater J. (2016). Learning serial constraint-based grammars. In J. J. McCarthy & J. Pater, eds., *Harmonic Grammar and Harmonic Serialism*. London: Equinox, pp. 369–88.

Strother-Garcia, K. (2019). Using Model Theory in Phonology: A Novel Characterization of Syllable Structure and Syllabification. PhD thesis. University of Delaware.

Strother-Garcia, K., Heinz, J. & Hwangbo, H. J. (2016). Using model theory for grammatical inference: A case study from phonology. In S. Verwer, M. van Zaanen & R. Smetsers, eds., *Proceedings of the Thirteenth International Conference on Grammatical Inference*, PMLR 57, pp. 66–78. https://proceedings.mlr.press/v57/strother-garcia16.html.

Tesar, B. (1995). Computational Optimality Theory. PhD thesis. University of Colorado, Boulder.

Tesar, B. (1998). Using the mutual inconsistency of structural descriptions to overcome ambiguity in language learning. In P. N. Tamanji & K. Kusumoto, eds., *Proceedings of the Twenty-Eighth Annual Meeting of the North East*

Linguistic Society, Vol. 1. Amherst, MA: Graduate Linguistics Student Association, pp. 469–83.

Tesar, B. (2007). Learnability. In P. de Lacy, ed., *The Cambridge Handbook of Phonology*. Cambridge: Cambridge University Press, pp. 555–74.

Tesar, B. (2014). *Output-Driven Phonology: Theory and Learning*. Cambridge: Cambridge University Press.

Tesar, B. (2017). Phonological learning with output-driven maps. *Language Acquisition*, 24(2), 148–67.

Tesar, B., Alderete, J., Horwood, G., Merchant, N., Nishitani, K. & Prince, A. (2003). Surgery in language learning. In G. Garding & M. Tsujimura, eds., *Proceedings of the Twenty-Second West Coast Conference on Formal Linguistics*. Somerville, MA: Cascadilla, pp. 477–90. https://doi.org/10.7282/T3Z036GP.

Tesar, B. & Prince, A. (2007). Using phonotactics to learn phonological alternations. In J. Cihlar, A. Franklin, D. Kaiser & J. Kimbara, eds., *Proceedings of the Thirty-Ninth Conference of the Chicago Linguistic Society*, Vol. 2. Chicago, IL: Chicago Linguistic Society, pp. 241–71.

Tesar, B. & Smolensky, P. (1993). The Learnability of Optimality Theory: An Algorithm and Some Basic Complexity Results. Master's thesis. University of Colorado, Boulder. ROA-2. http://ruccs.rutgers.edulroa.html.

Tesar, B. & Smolensky, P. (1996). *Learnability in Optimality Theory*. Technical report 96–3, Department of Cognitive Science, Johns Hopkins University. ROA-156. http://ruccs.rutgers.edulroa.html.

Tesar, B. & Smolensky, P. (1998). Learnability in optimality theory. *Linguistic Inquiry*, 29(2), 229–68.

Tesar, B. & Smolensky, P. (2000). *Learnability in Optimality Theory*. Cambridge, MA: MIT Press.

Tessier, A.-M. (2007). Biases and Stages in Phonological Acquisition. PhD thesis. University of Massachusetts, Amherst.

Tessier, A.-M. (2009). Frequency of violation and constraint-based phonological learning. *Lingua*, 119(1), 6–38.

Tessier, A.-M. (2012). Error-driven learning in harmonic serialism. In S. Keine & S. Sloggett, eds., *Proceedings of the Forty-Second Annual Meeting of the North East Linguistic Society*. Amherst, MA: Graduate Linguistics Student Association.

Tessier, A.-M. (2017). Learnability and learning algorithms in phonology. *Oxford Research Encyclopedia in Linguistics*.

Tessier, A.-M. & Jesney, K. (2014). Learning in harmonic serialism and the necessity of a richer base. *Phonology*, 31(1), 155–78.

Thorburn, C., Lau, E. & Feldman, N. (2022). A reinforcement learning approach to speech category acquisition. In Y. Gong & F. Kpogo, eds., *Proceedings of the Forty-Sixth Boston University Conference on Language Development*, Vol. 2. Somerville, MA: Cascadilla, pp. 797–811. www.lin gref.com/bucld/46/BUCLD46-60.pdf.

Valiant, L. (1984). A theory of the learnable. *Communications of the ACM*, 27(11), 1134–42. https://doi.org/10.1145/1968.1972.

Valiant, L. (2013). *Probably Approximately Correct: Nature's Algorithms for Learning and Prospering in a Complex World*. New York: Basic Books.

Vaux, B. (2008). Why the phonological component must be serial and rule-based. In B. Vaux & A. Nevins, eds., *Rules, Constraints, and Phonological Phenomena*. Oxford: Oxford University Press, pp. 20–60.

Vaysse, O. (1986). Addition molle et fonctions p-locales. *Semigroup Forum*, 34, 157–75.

Vitevitch, M. S. & Luce, P. A. (1998). When words compete: Levels of processing in perception of spoken words. *Psychological Science*, 9(4), 325–9.

Vitevitch, M. S., Luce, P. A., Charles-Luce, J. & Kemmerer, D. (1997). Phonotactics and syllable stress: Implications for the processing of spoken nonsense words. *Language and Speech*, 40(1), 47–62.

Vu, M. H., Shafiei, N. & Graf, T. (2019). Case assignment in TSL syntax: A case study. In G. Jarosz, M. Nelson, B. O'Connor & J. Pater, eds., *Proceedings of the Society for Computation in Linguistics*, Vol. 2, Article 28. https://scholar works.umass.edu/scil/vol2/iss1/28.

Wang, Y. & Hayes, B. (2022). Learning underlying representations: Expectation maximization and the KK hierarchy. Poster presented at the Annual Meeting on Phonology. University of California, Los Angeles, October 21–23.

Washington, J., Ipasov, M. & Tyers, F. (2012). A finite-state morphological transducer for Kyrgyz. In N. Calzolari, K. Choukri, T. Declerck, M. U. Doğan, B. Maegaard, J. Mariani, A. Moreno, J. Odijk & S. Piperidis, eds., *Proceedings of the Eighth International Conference on Language Resources and Evaluation*. Istanbul: ELRA, pp. 934–40. www.lrec-conf .org/proceedings/lrec2012/pdf/1077_Paper.pdf.

Wieczorek, W. (2017). *Grammatical Inference: Algorithms, Routines and Applications*. New York: Springer.

Wilson, C. (2003). Analyzing Unbounded Spreading with Constraints: Marks, Targets, and Derivations. Master's thesis. University of California, Los Angeles.

Wilson, C. & Gallagher, G. (2018). Accidental gaps and surface-based phonotactic learning: A case study of South Bolivian Quechua. *Linguistic Inquiry*, 49(3), 610–23.

Wilson, C. & Obdeyn, M. (2009). Simplifying subsidiary theory: Statistical evidence from Arabic, Muna, Shona, and Wargamay. Master's thesis. Johns Hopkins University.

Wu, K. & Heinz, J. (2023). String extension learning despite noisy intrusions. In F. Coste, F. Ouardi & G. Rabusseau, eds., *Proceedings of the Sixteenth International Conference on Grammatical Inference*. PMLR 217, pp. 80–95. https://proceedings.mlr.press/v217/wu23a.html.

Yang, C. (2016). *The Price of Linguistic Productivity: How Children Learn to Break the Rules of Language*. Cambridge, MA: MIT Press.

Yip, M. (1989). Contour tones. *Phonology*, 6(1), 149–74.

Zuraw, K. (2000). Patterned Exceptions in Phonology. PhD thesis. University of California, Los Angeles.

Zymet, J. (2018). Lexical Propensities in Phonology: Corpus and Experimental Evidence, Grammar, and Learning. PhD thesis. University of California, Los Angeles.

Zymet, J. (2019). Learning a frequency-matching grammar together with lexical idiosyncrasy: MaxEnt versus hierarchical regression. In K. Hout, A. Mai, A. McCollum, S. Rose & M. Zaslansky, eds., *Proceedings of the 2018 Annual Meeting on Phonology*. Washington, DC: Linguistic Society of America. https://doi.org/10.3765/amp.v7i0.4495.

Phonology

Robert Kennedy

University of California, Santa Barbara

Robert Kennedy is a Senior Lecturer in Linguistics at the University of California, Santa Barbara. His research has focused on segmental and rhythmic alternations in reduplicative phonology, with an emphasis on interactions among stress patterns, morphological structure, and allomorphic phenomena, and socio-phonological variation within and across the vowel systems of varieties of English. His work has appeared in *Linguistic Inquiry*, *Phonology*, and *American Speech*. He is also the author of *Phonology: A Coursebook* (Cambridge University Press), an introductory textbook for students of phonology.

Patrycja Strycharczuk

University of Manchester

Patrycja Strycharczuk is Senior Lecturer in Linguistics and Quantitative Methods at the University of Manchester. Her research programme is centered on exploring the sound structure of language by using instrumental articulatory data. Her major research projects to date have examined the relationship between phonology and phonetics in the context of laryngeal processes, the morphology–phonetics interactions, and articulatory dynamics as a factor in sound change. The results of these investigations have appeared in journals such as *Journal of Phonetics*, *Laboratory Phonology*, and *Journal of the Acoustical Society of America*. She has received funding from the British Academy and the Arts and Humanities Research Council.

Editorial Board

About the Series

Cambridge Elements in Phonology is an innovative series that presents the growth and trajectory of phonology and its advancements in theory and methods, through an exploration of a wide range of topics, including classical problems in phonology, typological and aerial phenomena, and interfaces and extensions of phonology to neighbouring disciplines.

Cambridge Elements ☰

Phonology

Elements in the Series

Coarticulation in Phonology
Georgia Zellou

Complexity in the Phonology of Tone
Lian-Hee Wee and Mingxing Li

Quantitative and Computational Approaches to Phonology
Jane Chandlee

A full series listing is available at: www.cambridge.org/EPHO

Printed in the United States
by Baker & Taylor Publisher Services